The Organized Musician

Debbie Stanley

The Organized Musician

Print:
ISBN: 0-9852768-6-X
ISBN-13: 978-0-9852768-6-7

E-book:
ISBN: 0-9852768-7-8
ISBN-13: 978-0-9852768-7-4

DEDICATION

A) Yep, that's what it takes.

B) To every musician who has said, "Organized? Pfff I wish…."

ACKNOWLEDGMENTS

Every musician, industry professional, and fellow music fan I've met has taught me something, intentionally or not, and I'm grateful for all of it. Here are some of my most valued teachers:

Jesse Atwell, Jeff Babbitt, Roggie Baer, Taylor Baker, Scott Baumann, Brady Beal, Chris Bell, Emily Bell, Stephanie Bergara, Brady Blade, Stefan Bouts, Mark Bradford, Jack Burton, Elizabeth Cawein, Victor Celania, Barry Coffing, Cody Cowan, Annette Crawford, Michael Culbertson, Kevin Curtin, Brandon DeMaris, Jennifer Dugas, Chris Dye, Dustin Edwards, CJ Eiriksson, Ulrich Ellison, John Evans, Daniel Eyes, Laurie Gallardo, Jon Garrett, Bobby Garza, Ben George, Jimmy George, Kelly Goldstein, John Guertin, Helen Haake, Michael Hale, Edward Hamell, Malcolm Harper, Eric Harrison, Jennifer Houlihan, Kate Howard, Michael Ingber, Erin Ivey, Terrany Johnson, Gregory Kallenberg, Charlie Karls, Donovan Keith, Colin Kendrick, Jason Kloess, Ange Kogutz, Dino Kovas, Nancy LaBarbiera, Kris Lager, Adrienne Lake, Nick Landis, Rakefet Laviolette, Jimi Lee, Dean Lofton, Loris Lowe, Walker Lukens, Sean Makra, James Mason, Christian McNeill, David Messier, Michael Milligan, Lawrence "Boo" Mitchell, Maegan Morace, Zack Morgan, Ryan Morris, Jon Niess, Andy Nolte, Matt Ott, Michelle Patronella, Alex Peterson, Deanna Peterson, Glenn Peterson Jr., Glenn Peterson Sr., Don Pitts, Sam Powell, Amy Price, Ray Prim, Barbara Rappaport, Nakia Reynoso, Mike Roberts, Nate Rodriguez, Tracey Schulz, Dianne Scott, Ken Shepherd Sr., Loren Shie, Glenn Smith, Sunni Soper, Darlene Starr, Cari Hutson St. Marie, Earl Thomas, Alex Vallejo, Andrea Villarreal, Heather Wagner Reed, Shane Walden, Drew Walker, Tyler Wallace

ABOUT THE AUTHOR

Debbie Stanley has been a self-employed organizational consultant since 1997. She has degrees in journalism, industrial/organizational psychology, and mental health counseling, and enjoys translating the eye-glazing rhetoric of her scholarly education into concepts that make sense in everyday life. She's been devoted to helping musicians get their act together since moving to Austin, Texas, in 2012. Contact her at www.ThoughtsInOrder.com and facebook.com/ThoughtsInOrder.

CONTENTS

INTRODUCTION

This book is for people who are dead serious about a career in music. If it's a want but not a need for you—if there's some other career you could be happy with, or if you're only interested in doing music if it's not too much of a hassle—you're meant to shine at something else. Don't waste your time here.

More specifically, this is for dead-serious independent musicians, whether you want to stay indie your whole career or you eventually want a label deal. Either way you must begin as a self-employed musician, which makes you a small business owner. You need business skills on top of your musical ability, at least to get started. You might eventually hire management, booking, and PR support, but at first, you have to do it all yourself, and that requires organization.

There's a persistent myth that creative people aren't capable of being organized and that they shouldn't try to be because it will interfere with their creativity. False. The musicians I know who are succeeding, however they define success, have organization around them, either self-created or hired out. Organization doesn't interfere with your creativity—it's lack of organization that makes you irritated, distracted, preoccupied, and blocked.

How to Use This Book

The Organized Musician is structured from fundamentals to performance. Like learning music, that's one way, but not the only way, to learn organization.

You can jump ahead to Section 3 and get right into using the tools, same as when I found sheet music for "Ode to Joy" in my grandma's piano bench and figured out which keys matched those notes. But since I'm not a natural musician, I didn't infer anything about how music works from that simple exercise. I was just mimicking.

Similarly, if you're not a naturally organized person, you won't learn how to be organized by using a few tools out of context. To really understand what you're doing, you'll want to read Sections 1 and 2 on Fundamentals and Strategic Choices. The chapters in both of those sections start with concepts that you can apply across a variety of situations and end with quick takeaways you can use immediately.

It's like the difference between learning notes or beats and learning feel. Some people have great feel from the beginning and just need to learn the specifics of how to make the right sounds with their instrument; others start with the mechanics and develop expressiveness as they go. Whichever way you do it, you need both elements to be a true musician—or to be truly organized.

SECTION 1: FUNDAMENTALS

There's "getting organized," and then there's being organized. You do the first to set yourself up for a lifetime of the second.

It's not like what you see on TV. That type of organizing is both overdramatized and oversimplified. In real life, the process doesn't have to include screaming, crying, or agonized parting with cherished belongings, and it rarely leads to a glorious reveal. In fact, it's more about organizing things you can't see—time and information—than it is about objects. There is no finale, because it never actually ends ... it just becomes less work over time.

Organization is the same as success in the music business: Once you get there, you have to keep working to stay there. Also like music, the fundamentals that you learn in the beginning continue to serve you for the rest of your life. As you build skill and confidence, your comprehension of the fundamentals deepens, your creativity thrives, and you become better able to innovate or even break the rules.

The first section of *The Organized Musician* introduces the fundamentals of organizing theory. These are universal principles, so they apply to every industry and every life, but in this book I'm offering them in context for musicians and music industry professionals. Once we've got this foundation in place, we'll move on to strategizing and then to systems and tools.

CHAPTER 1:

TIME

I'm not going to ease you into this. We're tackling the hardest part first.

The most essential organizational skill for a DIY musician is time management. Organizing your data and your belongings are important too, but those also require first organizing your time. If you get to the gig 30 minutes before load-in and your gear is tangled and strewn all over your vehicle, you're still better off than if you show up tidy and inventoried and 30 minutes late. Being cluttery stresses you, and you can fix it when you get fed up with it, but being late stresses the venue and can burn bridges that you won't be able to repair. Taking control of your time is your most important objective.

Time is also the hardest thing to organize, because it doesn't stay organized. You can put your books on a shelf or your clothes in the closet and they'll stay where you put them until someone moves them. Not so with time: Every day you have to reorganize it.

To make it even harder, you have to manage different sequences of time all at once—your daily tasks, projects for the month, plans for the year, and goals for your lifetime all need your attention, often simultaneously.

So that's what we're up against here. It's daunting but conquerable. Let's start with some concepts to help you get your head around this challenge.

"Spending" Time

Time is like money. They're both forms of currency, and often one replaces the other: If you don't have money, you'll have to spend time. When you're indie and still developing, you don't have the money to pay for everything you need, so you do it yourself. You spend your time. Once you get some money, you start paying people to do some of the work for you. You buy back your time.

The big problem with time as a form of currency is that it's limited. On one hand, it's great that you get a free stipend of time every day. You don't have to do anything to receive it—it simply appears as a deposit in your time bank, 24 new hours every midnight.

On the other hand, there is nothing you can do to receive more time. It is literally impossible. Think of all the language we have around this: make time, find time, stretch time, gain time, save time. These are all illusions. You get the same amount of time as everyone else, on the same schedule, in the same increments.

This illusion of a bottomless well of time is a major pitfall for ambitious indie artists. You go to a workshop or read a book or meet with a consultant, learn dozens of great ways to grow your music business, get all fired up and motivated, and tell yourself you're going to do all of those things. All it will take is commitment and self-discipline and focus and effort, and you have those qualities so you can do this!

No. You can't do all of it. The math doesn't work. Enacting every great idea would take more hours than you have. You must choose the best ones that will fit your time budget.

You understand this easily when we're talking about money. Suppose you love vinyl and you're in the record store, calculating how many you can afford that day. Or you need strings or a cymbal or a pedal and you're in the gear store or on the website, calculating how much you can afford that day. You do this naturally, automatically. To master your time, you have to treat it the same as money.

So the first thing to understand is that time is like money: It's finite. Next is recognizing that, of your already limited time, you only have authority over a portion of it.

Externally vs. Internally Controlled Time

All of your time is either externally or internally controlled. Externally controlled time is governed by other people or circumstances. Sleep is the one form of externally controlled time that everyone has. As the operator of a human body, you have no choice here. Sleep is a requirement of survival. Beyond that, externally controlled time is the hours you must spend at your day job, or at school, or commuting—obligations that you really can't afford not to fulfill. It's also all of the time that you've voluntarily committed to someone or something else: Ancillary things like playing in a sports league or taking a regular shift at the animal shelter, but also all of your music-related commitments: rehearsals, performances, recording sessions, media appearances, songwriting circles. Anything with a deadline or a schedule becomes externally controlled time as soon as you promise to do it.

Internally controlled, or self-controlled, time is what's left. It's what we tend to call "free time," which is ridiculous since, as you can now see, it's not at all free or cheap. Your internally controlled time—the time you get to use exactly how you want to use it—is a scarce and precious resource.

Let's look at the numbers.

Budgeting Your Time

You can't know how much money you can spend until you know how much you have. It's the same with time. So the first step of creating a time budget is to audit your current time usage. I know this part's a drag. Hang in there … it's worth it.

Start by looking at an average week:

1. Total the amount of sleep you get per week. If you don't normally keep track of this, take a guess for now.
2. List your external time commitments, including time spent preparing or commuting, and the number of hours you spend on each. (Again, guess for now if needed.) Then total the hours spent on each. This plus your sleep time is your average externally controlled time per week.
3. Complete this equation: 168 hours in a week minus [hours slept per week] minus [other externally controlled hours per week] = your internally controlled hours per week

Example: Suppose you're a singer/songwriter with a full-time day job. Single, no kids, and no time commitments to any teams or groups. You've done a few open mics, been included in some well-received showcases, and you want to start getting regular bookings around town. Here's what your hours look like right now: 168 – 56 (sleep) – 55 (day job + commute) = 57.

Well, cool ... 57 hours sounds like plenty of time to get things done, right? Eh, not really. Within this internally controlled time, you have to eat, take care of personal hygiene, do laundry, pay bills, do your household chores and shopping, and deal with all the annoying little things that pop up in everyone's life (the car breaks down, you get the flu, your mom needs you to dog-sit, the A/C goes out, and on and on). And also within this time, you're supposed to exercise and find time to relax.

Suppose all of that looks like this:

- Meals: 7 hrs
- Hygiene/grooming: 7 hrs
- Laundry/household chores: 3 hrs
- Shopping: 2 hrs
- Exercise: 3 hrs
- Downtime: 7 hrs
- Annoying stuff: 3 hrs

Now your internally controlled time is down to 25 hours per week.

Here's another important reality: Take out an additional, say, 2 hours per week because all of these things don't fit neatly side by side in your days. There are little bits of time that leak out and are wasted in between each of these. So now you're at 23 hours per week, or about 3 hours per day, to build your music career. That's both the admin time to get the gigs and the additional performance time once you get them. And remember, this is for a single person with no kids and no commitments beyond a day job.

Sobering, huh?

You could give up at this point. Or you can get even more serious about making careful choices with your time.

Deciding What to Do Each Day

There are key differences among values and goals, projects and tasks, and urgent and important items. It's essential that you define each one correctly and remember those distinctions from now until forever: That's how you keep your thoughts organized and get back on track when you're disoriented and have temporarily lost your way.

Values vs. goals:

Your values come from your beliefs and morals. They're not necessarily reflected in your behavior, though, and that causes internal conflict. If you value creative expression but you hit a point in your life when you're not doing anything creative, you'll feel it somehow—sadness, restlessness, irritability, or just as if something's missing. If you value being an honest person but you do something dishonest, you'll feel guilty and maybe also anxious, angry, or defeated. These reactions will happen even when you have a solid reason for acting in conflict with your values. If music is your passion but you had to set it aside to make more money or until the kids are grown, you'll still long for it.

Values can change over time. A common example is people who valued money very highly in the early years of their career but eventually came to value something else even more: enjoying their work, having time for family or hobbies, doing work that helps others. When you realize your values have evolved and you act on it, or when you realize you have a value that you haven't been acting on, the resulting life changes can be pretty dramatic.

Values and goals are different but connected. Values are how you want to be and goals are what you want to do. If they're not in alignment—if your goals don't give you ways to act on your values—you won't have the drive to achieve those goals. If you do happen to achieve an ill-fitting goal (e.g. a degree or job in a field that was your parents' passion but not yours) and even if you make a career out of it, it won't be the life you really wanted all along. This is where deathbed regrets come from.

We'll talk more about values and goals in Chapter 5: Direction.

Projects vs. tasks:

A project is a set of tasks. Very large projects have sub-projects, which are still just simply sets of tasks. Musicians often refer to their band as "the project"; if they're in more than one band, they're involved with more than one project.

Sometimes we misinterpret the term "project" by giving it a negative connotation. When we say, "Aww man, that's gonna be a project," we mean it's a huge and probably unpleasant job, which mischaracterizes the concept. "Project" is about number of steps and overall scope, not about difficulty or importance.

The problem with misconstruing the word "project" is that it overworks the word "task." If a so-called task has more than one step, it's a project. Perhaps a very small project; not something you would think of as "a project," but because we misuse the word "project," we fail to call it what it is. We call it a task and then beat ourselves up for not doing it.

Think about what happens when you put "Do laundry" on your to-do list and then skip it, or get as far as washing but forget to dry, or get as far as drying but don't fold or hang, so you have to do it all over again. Laundry is actually one of the most complex household chores. One does not simply "do the laundry" in a single step. It's a project, not a task.

Another key difference here is "simple" vs. "easy." They're not synonymous. We tend to think of projects as hard and tasks as easy. It's more accurate to recognize that, by definition, projects are complex, even if they're easy, and tasks are simple, even if they're difficult.

Soundcheck is always a complex project, even though for a skilled engineer it's usually easy. The task of telling a bandmember he's fired (one step in the project of replacing a bandmember) is simple but usually still difficult.

When you procrastinate on a task, it could be because it is simple but you know it won't be easy. More often, though, it's because the item is actually a project and you haven't broken it down enough to figure out where to start. If you use a to-do list already, are there items that you keep skipping? Look at that list and consider whether those lingering "tasks" are actually projects.

Urgent vs. important:

Understanding this distinction will keep you in charge of deciding what to do each day and choosing tasks that contribute to your goals instead of having stuff simply happen. This is the thought pattern that makes people proactive and not just reactive.

Like "simple" and "easy," this is another pair of terms that are often used interchangeably but are not synonymous. Urgent means time-sensitive. Important means it has consequences. There are four possible combinations of these characteristics:

- Urgent but not important: This is an enormous pitfall. How often do you respond to something that has a sense of urgency but turned out to be unimportant? Almost every distraction, interruption, and notification on your phone is urgent—it grabs your attention—but ultimately not important. If you were working on something important and some random urgency broke your concentration, it just cost you valuable time and energy. Allow that to happen often enough and you might look back and realize that cat videos tanked your career.

- **Important but not urgent:** These are the things you keep meaning to get around to. You know you need to do it, or should be doing it regularly, but you put it off. It hasn't become urgent yet, so it's easy to overlook or push aside in favor of a squeakier wheel. With better organization and a clear awareness of where the project is going and what the next step is, you'll be better able to motivate yourself to do these things without a formal deadline or an eye-opening crisis.

- **Neither urgent nor important:** This is the stuff musicians commonly do to kill time on the road or between soundcheck and the show. There is room for some of this in every life. In fact, you could say that a certain amount of downtime doing unimportant things is important in the grand scheme of things. But, like Skittles or bourbon or expensive guitars or whatever your vice is, you need a limit. Those limbo times on the road and backstage can be used for email, social media, advance prep for upcoming shows, gear maintenance, merch organizing, and the other million little tasks you will always have.

- **Both urgent and important:** This is the least common of the four combos. A great recurring example for musicians is hitting your call times, whether to load-in or the stage or the studio. It's urgent because it's a deadline, and it's important because it's your reputation. If you're late more than 10% of the time, people do notice (both bandmates and venues) and it affects their opinion of your reliability and professionalism. If you think it's OK to show up late because the sound guy won't be ready anyway or you don't have that much to load in or you have the farthest drive or whatever—no matter the reason, you're wrong. Bands known for being late get passed over for gigs, and often they never even know they were considered and disregarded. Smart bandleaders fire even highly talented players if they're chronically late.

Big rocks first:

There's a demonstration that time management consultants use when speaking to live audiences. The speaker takes a water pitcher, loads it up with softball-sized rocks, and asks the audience, "Is it full?" They of course say yes. Then the speaker grabs a container of pebbles and pours them into the pitcher, filling in the spaces around the big rocks. Again the speaker asks, "Is it full?" and the audience, not wanting to get played again, says, "Umm ... yes?"

Next the speaker pours in sand. This time the audience refuses to commit to the pitcher's fullness. Lastly, the speaker pours in water, up to the very top, and now, finally, the audience shouts, "Yes! It's really full!" And it is. So the speaker pours out that whole mess, refills the pitcher with just water, and asks, "What would happen if you tried to put in the big rocks now?"

They wouldn't fit, obviously. The big rocks have to go in first if they're going to make it in at all.

The point of the lesson is this: The big rocks are your important but usually not urgent life priorities. They need to go into your schedule first and stay there. Let the little stuff flow in around them.

●

With all of this in mind, you'll be able to create a daily to-do list that covers all of the menial little tasks of life and also moves you forward on your music projects. We'll get into this in detail in Section 2, with chapters on strategic planning in various aspects of the music biz.

The 80/20 Rule

You can't always know which time expenditures will pay off. Most of what you do will, at best, contribute in some small way to moving the entire operation forward. At worst, it will knock you back.

There is a theory called the Pareto Principle, a.k.a. the 80/20 Rule, that tells us, on average, 20% of any category is the really valuable stuff, and the other 80% is of less value. Some people take this to mean that 80% of everything is crap. That's an exaggeration: the 80% isn't all useLESS. Some of it is, but most of it is just less useFUL.

The 80/20 Rule applies to belongings (about 20% of your clothes are in heavy rotation), data (about 20% of your songs are the strongest), people (around 20% of your supporters are potentially the superfans who give you money and free promotion), and time: 20% of the time you spend pays off big.

Once you're aware of it, you can use this theory in so many ways. First and most important, when you start to evaluate things through this lens, you can sometimes identify which portion of a category is the 20%. It's not always possible: With time expenditures, you often won't know until afterwards which efforts were the most fruitful. But if you're tracking the results of those efforts, going forward you can better anticipate which uses of your time will result in the greatest gains.

Another valuable use of this theory is to assess the 80%. We all have useless stuff, and this is where you'll find it. This does not mean you should scrap 80% of everything! But it's likely that some of it should go. When you whittle down your 80%s across all the categories of your life, you'll still have that 80/20 ratio, but all of it will be more valuable than before.

One Loophole

Those expressions we reviewed earlier—save time, make time, find time—are all illusions, but there is one that provides a loophole: You can, in a sense, "buy time" from other people and you have two ways to do it: with money or with another form of currency known as "relationship equity." The good news about relationship equity is that you can earn an unlimited amount of it, and you can accumulate it much more easily than money. We'll explore this more in Chapter 7: Relationships.

•

Organization is built with habits. Let's finish this chapter with some time-related ones:

Habits That Waste Your Time

Failing to define your goals:

You didn't just throw a dart at a board full of industries, land on "music," and accept it with a shrug. You chose music over all other options because it's your passion, but you must define it more specifically than that. What part of the music industry? What role do you want? If it's performance, what instrument? What genre? Touring or local only? Where, how often, and to what size of audiences? And dozens more questions. If you don't know exactly what you're aiming at, it's as if you're throwing darts blindfolded and hoping a bullseye will jump in front of them. More on goal-setting in Chapter 5: Direction.

Losing sight of your priorities:

It's so easy to take your eyes off the prize. It happens frequently if you live in reaction mode instead of actively planning your steps. But even if you're utterly fixated on achieving your goals, you might still be vulnerable if another captivating thing—or person—enters your life. Vocalist/songwriter Donovan Keith alludes to this risk in the mournful "Silhouette," about an enchanting girl "and the promises you made me forget." Here's a jarring realization: Having this career requires not having a multitude of other good things. There are difficult crossroads in your future.

Mishandling distractions:

This is the minute-by-minute version of forgetting your priorities. If you're supposed to be concentrating on those booking emails or that website update, but as you're working on it you keep checking Facebook or wandering away for a snack, you're just making everything harder for yourself and spending more time than you can afford. I trained myself out of this habit with a Nike "Just Do It" poster next to my computer. I cursed at the damn poster countless times, but it kept me on task. Here's another trick for when your brain keeps interrupting you with reminders of other things you want or need to do: Make a "parking lot" to jot them down and keep going. It could be a pad of sticky notes, a notebook, a note in an app on your phone—whatever method you can use to capture the thought and go right back to work without breaking your concentration.

Reinventing the wheel:

The most foolhardy myth about time that we nonetheless keep telling ourselves is, "I'll remember." Any time you do something that you're going to do again, document the procedure. Make a checklist. Capture the details of the steps as you're doing them so the process can go even more quickly and accurately the next time. Then remember to use the checklist next time, and refine or correct it. Soon you'll have a killer procedures manual and it will be far easier to delegate tasks to others.

Having "one-more-thing-itis":

This is my cute name for trying to do just one more thing before you leave. It's a foolproof way to make yourself late. This habit isn't just about wanting to get more done—it's about fearing that you won't remember to do it later. If you find yourself regularly "one more thing"ing it, try this: In the last half-hour before you're supposed to leave, instead of doing those supposedly quick little things that pop into your head, write them down. For ideas that occur to you at home as you're getting ready, keep a dry-erase marker near your mirror and jot them right on the glass. Your notes will be there when you get back and they'll wipe off with a tissue when you're done with them. (Shoutout to dance instructor Mike Roberts for that genius idea!) At work, write them on a pad or on sticky notes that you can leave in your workspace or put in your pocket. Getting disciplined about this might be the one change that converts you from chronically late to usually on time.

Practicing perfectionism:

There are very few things in life that you need to do perfectly, including organization. There is such a thing as "organized enough." You can get an A without getting 100%, so unless 99% is going to cause irreparable harm, aim for the A. One of my favorite sayings is, "Perfect is the enemy of good."

Creating self-inflicted do-overs:

On the flip side of perfectionism, you need to do a good enough job to keep from having to do the danged thing over again. Don't cut corners when it's likely to cost you time, money, or opportunity. With any task that you're going to do more than once, take the time to develop a system so you can do it quickly and perhaps less attentively from then on and still get a good result. Booking pitch emails are a good example; more to come on that in Chapter 9: Booking & Touring.

Falling down digital rabbit holes:

Many of these—social media, email, web searching—are necessary for business but they're also tempting time sucks. Others like game apps and Netflix are just entertainment. (OK, yes, music documentaries are research.) With all of these, it's easy to sink into a daze and lose track of what you came to do and how much time you could afford. Distinguish when you're using them for business vs. relaxation, and make conscious choices about your time with each. Set a timer if you have to, or get into them only when you know some other force will pull you away, such as in the green room before a show or waiting your turn at the DMV.

Over-partying:

If you set aside time for a night out or hung out with fans after your show for the savvy purpose of building your following, but you drank or smoked so much that you're useless the next day, you mismanaged your time. Take it from drummer Alex Vallejo, whose band did all of the cliché stuff in their early years: The rock & roll lifestyle is incompatible with success as an indie musician. Get this out of your system quickly and stop making it that much harder for yourself.

Habits That Protect Your Time

Write down your Big Picture:

In a notebook, in a digital document, on a posterboard, on your mirror with a dry-erase marker ... whatever way works for you, but somewhere, in some form, have a clear description of your goals and the timeline and tasks that are carrying you toward them. Look at it whenever you're feeling unfocused or uninspired, and use it to get reoriented so that your tiny tasks have meaningful context.

Know your flow:

How long can you work without losing concentration? 15 minutes? An hour? Do you do better working on something a little bit each day, or in a full-day marathon? Or as career counselor Wilma Fellman asks, are you a sprinter or a plodder? Sprinters like to work on projects when inspiration hits (or a deadline looms), while plodders prefer to do a little at a time within a regular, methodical routine. Whichever you are, don't try to change: Embrace it and make it work for you.

Know your energy cycle:

Are you an earlybird, a night owl, or maybe the in-between afternoon person? Again, whichever you are, don't try to change. Studies indicate that this tendency is innate, not just a habit or a preference. Try to complete your tasks at the time of day when you're most likely to have the type of energy they require: Do email and write social media posts when you're best able to be quick and upbeat. Handle contracts and advances when you're sharpest and least likely to make errors. Do routine tasks like posting new shows to all of the online calendar platforms when you're most tolerant of boredom. Catch up on skimming social media timelines and checking out new music when you're fried and no good for much else anyway.

Recognize false urgencies:

The internet, and the email and smartphones it spawned, have conditioned us to respond with urgency to things that are utterly unimportant. Be very selective with who and what you turn on notifications for. Create periods of isolation when you can silence your phone and work offline, or if the work is web-based, open one browser window at a time. Close yourself in a room if your housemates need a visual cue not to disturb you. You might be surprised at how productive you can be without the constant pop-ups and dings.

Manage others' expectations:

When gates open at a festival or arena show, the barricades are already set up and the most enthusiastic fans run right up to them. Imagine how hard it would be to set up those fences if the crowds were already onsite. It's the same with your time commitments. Expressing your boundaries in advance is much easier than asserting them after they've already been crossed. If you need quiet time, tell your housemates. If you're not always available by phone/text/messenger, let people know so they don't think you're ignoring them. If you schedule something personal on a night that your band booker might add a gig, immediately block yourself out on the band calendar. If you're meeting with someone and you only have an hour, tell them in advance. If you're counting on someone to hit a deadline, tell them it's really a real deadline for real. This habit of being clear about your needs prevents interruptions, delays, and all sorts of interpersonal drama.

Commit slowly:

Some people have a self-defeating habit I call the "automatic yes." They regularly agree to things before thinking about whether they can actually do them. Other people hate it when you do this. They would much prefer that you say you'll think about it and get back to them, rather than saying yes and then bailing. So if you're a people-pleaser (as people with this habit tend to be), understand that the happiness you see on their faces when you say yes will be obliterated by the stress you cause them later when you fail to deliver. Instead of that knee-jerk yes response, say you'll look into whether you can do it, then look at your calendar and your workload and make a well-considered choice. If you come back with a yes after that, your commitment will have more credibility and you'll be much more likely to actually fulfill it.

Build in external accountability:

Having no one to answer to can be the best and the worst thing about self-employment. Bosses create deadlines, so if deadlines are what makes you get things done, you're at a disadvantage with self-directed activities like songwriting and recording. You can trick yourself into acting like you have a boss by creating external accountability: setting up situations where you must deliver by a deadline or it will cost you money, inconvenience others, or mightily embarrass you. Scheduling studio time is an example: When you've got the space, engineers, and musicians all booked, ya gotta show up with songs. Committing to deadlines can be a gut-wrenching way to get things done, but if adrenaline-soaked all-nighters are what works for you, you'll be glad you did it.

CHAPTER 2:

DATA

Let me say up front that, for most people, data is by far the most boring thing to organize. Even an org nerd like myself gets sick of it at some point. It's discouraging because your progress isn't as visually impactful as, say, organizing your basement. It can take an entire day to work through one box of papers, because that one box can require hundreds of decisions.

I'm going to make it more tolerable for you by starting with some concepts that will clarify what data actually is and show you your preferences right away, which will prevent wasting time down the road on systems that won't work for you.

Functional vs. Creative Data

When I say "data," I mean any form of information, created or captured in any possible way. Some obvious examples are identifiers (your name, social security number, logins & passwords), contacts (others' emails, phone numbers, social media handles), financial records, and performance statistics. These are all functional forms of data.

Some examples you might not immediately think of as data include all of your creations: music, album art, website, photos, videos, and social media posts. It might seem odd to refer to the fruits of your craft as data, but in the organizational sense, it is, so we'll distinguish it from the usual stuff by calling it creative data.

These two types of data are typically organized differently, but there can be some overlap between the two: When you're writing a song, the files (legal pads, voice recorder clips, Pro Tools tracks, etc.) are a set of creative data, but once it's completed and released, the song is now organized like functional data, even though it's still a creative asset. Recognizing that you can organize data in different ways depending on whether it's functional or creative frees you to have varying systems that make sense within your overall strategy.

Paper or Electronic?

When you're dealing with data, do you like paper, or do you wish you could get rid of it completely? It's important to know this about yourself because it directs all of your data organization strategies.

For functional data:

People who prefer paper for their functional data, or who think they hate it but end up reverting back to it over and over, tend to be tactile processors of information: They find that handwriting helps them to focus more than typing, and if they must type, they then print more often than non-tactile processors. They need to be able to literally hold the data in their hands. For these folks, digital information feels flat and distant, and that distance deadens their ability to fully engage with the info.

One of the clearest indicators of this preference is in how you manage appointments, contacts, and tasks. If you use a planner system, is it some sort of book, or is it an app? Before there were smartphones, and even earlier before electronic planners like the Blackberry and Palm Pilot, the state-of-the-art system was the Franklin Planner: A ring binder with paper pages sectioned into calendar, contacts, tasks, and notes. It was great for tactile processors, but it had serious flaws that digital eliminated, including limited data capacity, no quick search function, and no data backup.

Many people converted to digital and never missed their paper planner; others (myself included) switched to digital systems for their obvious advantages but still need to put pen to paper (or marker to dry-erase board) now and then to really feel connected to the data. And some folks remain staunch paper people, with a pocket calendar, handwritten to-do list, paper address book, or even an actual Franklin Planner (yes, they still make them).

For creative data:

Artists including musicians often handle functional and creative data differently. Even if you're fully engaged and comfortable with paperless scheduling and management of contacts, tasks, and files, you might still prefer to create by hand.

If you're a lyricist, do you compose initially on paper or on a device? If you play from sheet music or charts, does it feel different to work from an iPad screen vs. a printout or handwritten sheet? Which way feels more connected and less artificial for you, or are they pretty much the same?

If you do indeed prefer to handle creative data differently from functional data, keep this in mind when we get to strategies. It's fine to have some systems that are paper-based and some that are digital. The trick is making intentional, informed decisions about all of it and setting up systems that will continue to work together and make sense to you.

Paper is still here to stay:

Data organization is now mostly digital, but not completely. We're not yet a paperless world, so you still need to know how to manage your data in physical form in addition to conquering it electronically.

If you prefer paper over digital, you need systems for keeping it from overwhelming you. Admittedly, you won't get much sympathy—mostly you'll get people telling you to get a damn computer or learn how to use a smartphone or some other unhelpful criticism. If paper is what works for you, I encourage you to keep using it. Trying to do something your brain isn't wired for is a recipe for failure. At the same time, learn to use digital at least a little bit. It's definitely the way of the world now, so if you don't learn to engage with it in at least some basic ways, you will get left behind.

If you prefer digital over paper, you'll have a much easier time. Just be careful not to make hasty decisions you might regret, like digitizing all photos, posters, and books and getting rid of the paper copies. It might be the right choice for you, but then again you might be sorry later, so really think it through before you go paperless on both your functional and your creative or sentimental data.

Stuff Out or Stuff Away?

The preference for paper vs. digital can also be related to your visual preference: Whether you function better with things put away or left out in sight.

People tend to be either "stuff out" types or "stuff away" types. Stuff-outs would rather have things out in sight, for convenience (why put away the remote when I use it every night?), as memory prompts (Joe's CD is sitting there to remind me to give it to Becca), or to create a visual landscape rich with interesting and inspiring elements (that glass vase full of guitar picks). Stuff-aways prefer an uncluttered visual space. If they put away the remote every night, it's because seeing it sitting there the next morning will be distracting. They prefer visually unobtrusive systems for memory prompts: a note on the calendar entry for Becca's next show that says, "Take Joe's CD (in desk drawer)." If they have a vase of picks sitting out, it's because they find it especially pleasant to look at, not because they need it for inspiration or motivation, and it will likely be one of very few decorative elements in the space.

Most people can easily self-identify as a stuff-out or stuff-away, but here's an important note: You can't always tell which a person is by looking at his or her space. A clear, uncluttered space could indicate the person is a stuff-away, or it could indicate s/he is a tortured stuff-out living with a dominant stuff-away. A jam-packed, visual riot of a space could indicate a happily stuff-out person, or it could signify someone who is living in misery because s/he's such a staunch stuff-away that s/he doesn't know where to begin decluttering the space.

A stuff-out with a clear space and a stuff-away with a cluttered space are likely both feeling the same way: Distracted, frustrated, and unable to operate at peak capacity.

●

You can now think of data as either functional or creative (or in some cases both), and as either paper or digital, and you have an idea of how much your visual preference influences your paper vs. digital preference. Knowing this, you're better positioned to choose more compatible systems for organizing all of your data.

Have you noticed how data management intersects with time management? If you jot a sticky note instead of entering the info into an app, is it because you don't have (or feel like you don't have) time to "do it right"? If your desk is covered with papers but in your heart you're a stuff-away, is it because you haven't spent time creating systems for managing those papers?

Now let's look at some concepts you can use for clearing a backlog of data and setting up systems to deal with it into the future. This will position you for the strategies and systems sections coming up later.

Homes for Your Data

The concept of "homes" is perhaps the most foundational element of organizing theory. The idea is that in order to be organized, you have to designate a home for every one of your things (whether object, piece of data, or element of time). On the face of it, that sounds impossibly detailed, but it's actually not, because it's done in conjunction with another foundational organizing theory: Categorization. A further saving grace: Most of your stuff already has designated homes; you've just never thought of it that way.

Recognizing what the homes are will allow you to be more intentional about using them, and it will give you the information you need to finally put away those items that you don't know what to do with. I'll also show you how this works with tangible stuff in Chapter 3: Objects.

"Meta-decisions": Decisions about Deciding

This is my term for making decisions ahead of time about the categories of stuff you expect to find when you start sorting. "Meta" means "about itself," so a meta-decision is a decision about decision-making. This applies to objects too, but for now we'll look at how it works with data. In sorting boxes of old personal papers, common meta-decisions might include:

- "I'll toss all junk mail, coupons, and catalogs"
- "I'll toss all magazines more than one year old"
- "I'll shred all credit card offers"
- "I'll save all photos and look at them in detail later"

Meta-decisions keep you from spending too much time pondering each item. The worst part of sorting data is the tendency to get bogged down in each little decision. Meta-decisions apply some discipline to the process (no, I won't stop and look at just this one catalog, it's old and I know the website, I'll check it out later, moving on) and make it easier and quicker to drill down to the important stuff.

The Relentless Data Deluge

If you never feel overwhelmed by incoming data, you are some kind of superhuman. Or your phone and email accounts are broken. ;) Most people find organizing data to be about as manageable as counting fish in a fast-flowing river. If you've been getting by with piles on your desk or in your bag, skimming off the most crucial items in your email, and starting a lot of texts and calls with, "Hey, sorry it took so long to get back ... ," you can take some comfort in knowing that you're normal. You can also get ready to celebrate, because I have some techniques that will put you in much better control of your endless influx of data. We'll also look at what to do with the backlog of data you already have, but first, let's fix the breaks in the dam.

Keeping up with new input:

Time to make some lists! Think about the kinds of data you receive and group them into categories that make sense to you. Here are mine as an example:

Types of Data I Receive (Your Mileage May Vary)	
Email	Web link
Voicemail	Paper mail
Text message	Business card
Facebook message	Handout (flyer, postcard, one-sheet, form)
Photo (digital) or video	Book
Song file	Idea (from someone else, in conversation)
Song link	Idea (of my own)

There are occasional exceptions, but this covers the majority of the types of data I deal with. It's actually not that long of a list, eh? This is a great example of how grouping things into categories makes them easier to organize. Now instead of having to think about 7,000 things individually, I can think about just 14 categories which cover all 7,000 of those things.

Next, list all the places you can think of where you receive data. These are not the items' ideal homes, although they are where the items will sit around (and perhaps get forgotten) if you don't make a system for moving them along.

Identifying the ways that data infiltrates your life can be a huge relief. It's like having mice or crickets or whatever the most hated pest is in your area: You see them all over your home and at first you feel like they're coming at you from all angles, but with some investigating you can narrow down their access points to a manageable number.

Here's my list of data access points. Remember, these are just one person's example. Again, it's kinda surprising to see how few there actually are:

Where My Data Arrives	
Email inbox (emails and voicemail files)	Camera SD cards (my "real" cameras)
Text messages app	Desk (where all the paper lands)
Facebook Messenger app	Notebook/legal pad (mostly meeting notes)
Phone camera roll	Mirrors (I jot ideas with dry-erase marker)

This list is worth making even if you don't continue on and create actual homes for your data. Once you've got your access points identified, at least you know where you need to check periodically. You might also be able to combine or eliminate some of them. For example, if incoming paper might land on the table or the counter or your desk or in your car or in your bag, this can motivate you to stick with putting it in just one of those places every time.

Speaking of incoming paper, here's something to notice: In my list above, the first five arrival points (inbox, text app, FB app, camera roll, SD cards) happen passively, meaning if it's that kind of data, that's where it goes automatically. The last three (desk, notebook, mirrors) require some self-discipline: I have to transport the data to those places for them to arrive there. So if (ok, when) I leave papers in my car or on the kitchen table, or write notes somewhere other than in my notebook or on a mirror, I mess myself up and make it impossible for my system to do its job. But life happens sometimes, so when I get a break after things have fallen apart for a time, I go around and collect the bits & pieces I've left in the wrong places and get them back into the system.

It's normal to have to do this periodically. The trick is to make that catch-up pass frequently enough that your system is online most of the time.

Once you've got your data tucked into its arrival spots, what do you do with it from there? One of three things: You file it, act on it, or toss it.

The FAT system:

This is an ingeniously simple sorting method developed by Barbara Hemphill, creator of the Paper Tiger data management system.

In each of your arrival spots, sort the data into three categories: File, Act, and Toss. File is stuff you don't need to do anything with but you need to keep it for reference or as a record of something. Act is stuff you need to act on. Toss is stuff to get rid of (trash, recycling, shredding).

Deal with the Toss items first—throw them in the trash or recycling, or shred them if needed—and move right along to the File and Act items. These will go from their arrival spot to an action spot or a storage spot.

Creating Your Action and Storage Spots

You've gotten rid of the junk and your remaining data is cued up for the next step. Categories are still your good friend here; they'll keep you from reverting back to treating each item as a unique individual, which quickly becomes overwhelming and can motivate you to just leave it all for some other time.

Continue building your data management system by making two new lists: One of where you put items that need some kind of action and one of where you put items that just need to be saved for reference or for archival purposes.

Don't start working on the action items just yet ... that's another common pitfall that will distract you from focusing on the big picture and giving needed attention to all of the items, not just the few that jump out at you in the moment.

Continuing with myself as one example, here are my lists of where the Act and the File items go:

Where It Goes for Action	Where It Goes for Storage	
Calendar (appointments)	Calendar (notes during/after)	Password app
Asana task app*	Email folders*	Music streaming app
Shelf space*	Contacts	Paper files*
Someone else (delegated item)	Computer files*	Fire safe
	Quick notes app	Bookcases (books/CDs/DVDs)

Master categories:

My Action and Storage spots marked with an asterisk all use the same set of master categories. I set them up this way to make it easier to remember how I group information and not have to think so hard about where to put each new thing. I have eight master categories: Avocations, Career, Community, Family & Friends, Finance, Happiness, Health, and Household. Each of these has subfolders, and it gets pretty detailed so I won't list it all here. What's important is that these categories work for me because they're in my own language and grouped in sections that make sense to my mind. They might not work for you or anyone else. How you group things and which words you use to label them should always be intuitive to you, so the system will seem familiar even if you don't look at it for months or longer.

You don't have to come up with multipurpose master categories right away. I've been evolving mine for over half my life. If you only get as far as grouping things into a few basic folders, it will certainly be better than nothing. It's normal to keep adding to and changing your filing systems. The crucial part is maintaining the system. If you abandon it, you might have an easier time starting over, but in the meantime you will have no system and life will be unnecessarily difficult.

Action and storage spots:

Notice that my data has only four possible places to go to get some action (heh). That's a very manageable number. As long as I use the system, it's tough to lose things in so few places:

- Calendar: An appointment, event, or something else I have to attend at a specific date and time.
- Asana task app: Any other task, with or without a deadline.
- Shelf space: Items I've received in paper form that need some action or that I need to hold onto for a future in-person meeting or event.
- Someone else: Anything that I've delegated to someone else to do. In most cases, I have to keep track of it until it's done, so I make an Asana task to do that.

Data that's going to storage has more potential destinations:

- Calendar: I sometimes jot a few points from a meeting or event in the notes section of its calendar entry—not action items but things like who else was there, where the catering came from if it was notable, who ran sound if it was a show, and any other really random stuff that I might want to search back for.

- Email folders: I will admit that I don't do "inbox zero"—more on that in Chapter 8—but when I do go through and declutter my email, these folders are what I use to file emails I'm keeping.
- Contacts: This is the usual name, phone, email, and mailing address, but I also store any other miscellaneous info about a person in their contact record: Birthday, family members' names, where and when I met the person, who introduced us, MBTI type, vehicle info (for arranging clients' parking credentials), clothing sizes (shopping for friends, wardrobe for clients) ... anything other than data that needs to be encrypted, which goes in my password app (below). I sometimes even make a contact record when I "friend" someone on Facebook, even if I don't get their phone or email, so I can remember what the initial connection was.
- Computer files: These are grouped within those eight master categories, then subcategorized from there.
- Quick notes app: I have a basic notes app that I use to keep running lists that aren't exactly tasks, aren't tied to any one event or person, and aren't time-sensitive. It's things like TV shows and movies that people have told me to see. If an item doesn't fit into any of these other storage spots but it's still worth capturing, it goes in the notes app.
- Password app: This is where I keep logins, passwords, credit cards, social security numbers, and other sensitive info.
- Music streaming app: These make it so easy to save an artist or song and/or add to a playlist. I save a lot of music in Spotify to follow up on later—nothing with a deadline or a business purpose, just things I hear on the fly and like.
- Paper files: It's rare now, but I do have some things that I save in paper form. Usually, though, if something is worth saving, it's worth taking a photo to save digitally instead of keeping the paper original.
- Fire safe: This is where most of the paper worth saving goes: Birth certificate, passport, social security card, and other things considered "vital records."
- Bookcases: As digital as I am, I do still have several bookcases with actual books plus CDs, DVDs, and even a few vinyls (purely sentimental since I don't have a turntable).

Clearing a Data Backlog

Now that you have systems for your new incoming data, you can use the same techniques to make quicker decisions about what to do with old papers, emails, and computer files.

Let me caution you here. This is a point at which people will sometimes organize just for the sake of organizing, and that is a complete waste of time. Say you have three boxes of papers that you've been dragging around with you for the last few years. Why do you believe you need to organize them right now? Is this really the most important thing you could be doing with your time today?

If your first international tour starts in two months, so you need a passport, so you need your birth certificate, and you can't find your birth certificate but you think it's in one of these boxes, then yes, you need to deal with the boxes right now. And since you need to dig through them to at least find your birth certificate, you might as well put in the time to organize the rest of what's in there.

If you're just annoyed that the boxes exist and you want not to be annoyed anymore, fine, spend some time on them while you're motivated to do it. Just don't neglect anything more important. In other words, don't use organizing as a sophisticated form of procrastination.

The beauty of this system for bulk processing is that it breaks down your decisions into manageable layers. Combined with some well-designed meta-decisions, you're now positioned to blaze through those boxes of random papers and quickly salvage the important stuff. That is, if there is any important stuff. You might get through all three boxes and find that the only thing that mattered was your birth certificate and the rest can go. Score!!

When you're dealing with a larger volume of data, the process will be more time-consuming but the FAT system and meta-decisions will greatly streamline it. Applied to those three boxes of miscellaneous papers, the FAT system will generate the now-familiar categories but with larger stacks: One of items to keep for reference (File), one of items that reminded you to do something (Act), and one of stuff to get rid of (Toss). Then you'll further subdivide each category as needed until you're through all of it.

Toss and File will be fairly straightforward if you have already set up your filing systems (both paper and digital). Act, however, might be a bit stressful with a large quantity of data to dig through. Here are some tips to make dealing with your Act items more tolerable and productive:

- First, have a chat with yourself about what you can realistically accomplish with these items right now. Chances are you won't be able to immediately complete all of the actions they have reminded you to do. Promise that you will not torture yourself with trying to do all of these things all at once. Remember that just because you've rediscovered them doesn't make them urgent. Breathe in, breathe out.

- Look at each item one by one. Put a sticky note on it (or write directly on it) and jot what you need to do with it. Don't just say "Do This!" or "Follow Up" or "Call": Write exactly what you need to do, how you need to follow up, or who you need to call (name, title, and number) and why. If there is a real deadline (not a self-imposed/scolding deadline), write that on your note too. Do this for each item, and complete the entire pile before you actually start any of the actions. Seriously. If you interrupt yourself now, chances are you won't finish this sorting project.

- Resist the urge to just pile them back up and tell yourself that you know what you need to do. Why spend time figuring it out again the next time you read the document? Write down what you're thinking while you're thinking it.

- Once all of the Act items are annotated, now you can decide which ones to act on first. But after all of this, you'll probably want to stop for the day, and that's fine. You made good notes, so you can come back to it later and pick up where you left off.

- If you need to set the project aside for a day or more, bundle each category and label it (File, Act, Toss, or whatever subcategories you have) so you'll remember what you were doing when you return.

Once you get through that backlog, never … what? You thought I was going to say never let it happen again? Psh, it probably will happen again—if not with paper then with something else that will get pushed aside by some other urgency or crisis. That's normal life. No, what I was going to say is this: Once you get through that backlog, never forget that you can use your systems to get caught up when stuff happens. Living an organized life doesn't mean never having chaos—it means recovering from inevitable episodes of chaos with methodical confidence.

●

Let's finish this chapter with some smart do's and don'ts for data:

Habits That Defeat Your Data Management

Trusting your memory:

Seriously, don't. You will forget things and then you'll waste time and energy trying to remember, trying to find the info, or creating a new system because you forgot what you were doing with the old one. There is nothing superior or skilled or noble about using your memory instead of an external system.

Skimming off the easy stuff:

Answering the simplest and most recent emails and other messages will barely keep you afloat and it sure won't get you ahead. We all get into this survival mode sometimes, but eventually you need to get to the bottom of that inbox. If you find it unbearably stressful, try these tricks: Set a timer and make yourself do it for only five minutes at a time. Or give yourself a quota (say, five messages) and do only that number at one time. If you're avoiding old messages because you dread finding a missed deadline or someone who is angry or disappointed with you, remind yourself that the other person has almost certainly been in the same position. Forgive yourself for messing up, then dive in so it won't get worse with another day gone.

The OHIO rule:

This stands for Only Handle It Once. It's a stupid rule but it's still out there, misleading people in magazines and on the interwebs. The concept behind it is to drop an iron fist on procrastination, but all it really does is force you to be completely reactive instead of proactive about what you do, and when, and in what order. True story: I had a client who was entering her house through the back door because the mail came through a slot in the front door. She knew the gospel of OHIO, so she was being careful not to touch the mail before she was ready to answer every letter and pay every bill in one sitting. Don't laugh at her—laugh at the foolish system. Instead of OHIO, touch the data as often as you need to, but make some sort of progress on it every time, whether it's adding a note to it, putting it in your task list or calendar, giving it to someone else to deal with, or some other baby step.

Habits That Make Data Management Easier

Document the steps when you do something technical:

I have a Word doc of running notes on how my website works—not the basic posting and design stuff but the behind-the-scenes specs that I won't remember later, such as which companies are my registrar, host, and platform and why I chose them; notes from tech support calls; and steps for technical tasks I've figured out how to do. By funny coincidence, in the midst of writing this section I had to stop and open that very document to help a client with similar questions. There's no need for or benefit to keeping that kind of information in your head, as long as you have saved it in a reliable system.

Have a system for naming your files:

Develop file-naming conventions for yourself. This way, all of your various files will have some commonalities that will help you stay oriented no matter what file or folder list you're in. For example, as you accumulate photos from your shows, you could start the file name with the name of the venue, then use the date of the show (which might not be the same as the date of the file), then include the photographer's name so you can easily remember who gets the credit whenever you reuse that photo. Example:

Continental Club Austin 2015-09-12 Lopez.jpg
Continental Club Austin 2015-12-19 Josiah.jpg
Continental Club Austin 2016-04-08 Lopez.jpg
Continental Club Houston 2016-02-05 fan Kate Howard.jpg
Rustic 2016-05-14 fan Amy Merrill
Sam's Burger Joint 2015-09-11 Crawford
Sam's Burger Joint 2016-02-19 Crawford

Notice how I set the dates as year-month-day? That makes them sort in chronological order WITHIN alphabetical order. Fancy!

Use your phone as a scanner:

Smartphones now have cameras good enough to take the place of a document scanner. This avoids an equipment expense and vastly simplifies the process of sending signed contracts, revised stage plots, and handwritten setlists, or simply scanning a receipt or note to save digitally. Try photographing a document with your phone: Put the doc on a flat surface, avoid casting a shadow on it, and hold the phone perfectly horizontal so the page shape isn't distorted. After you get the shot, go to your camera roll and zoom in on the photo to make sure you can read the text. This technique still isn't adequate for items you're going to use for marketing (don't take a photo of a paper poster and share it as a promotional item), but it will cover you for most administrative needs.

Create a time-delay recycling system:

Some people seem to end up with a lot of data that they want to keep for "a little while," "just in case"—stuff like receipts, confirmation numbers, bill stubs, check carbons, bank statements, bar napkin phone numbers, etc. If this is you, here's a way to offload it as soon as you no longer need it. Create a set of 12 paper file folders or large envelopes and label them with the next 12 months. You can reuse these, so hand-write and cross out as many times as you need to over the years. Whenever you get a piece of that "just for a while" data, file it in the envelope or folder of the future month when you figure it will be safe to toss it if you haven't needed it by then. If you can't choose a date, put it out three months and re-evaluate it at that point. Then, with each new month, get rid of the contents of the last month's folder/envelope.

CHAPTER 3:

OBJECTS

I find it funny (and kind of exasperating) that the media equates organization almost solely with physical things and spaces: Closets, kitchen cabinets, garages, etc. I suppose it makes sense, since objects are the only aspect of organization that you can photograph and put on a magazine cover or use to kill an hour of cable TV ending with a big reveal, all with strategic new-product placement throughout. But still.

Organizing your belongings and your spaces is a very important part of being organized overall. Just don't believe the hype and start thinking that a zen-tidy kitchen with the perfect set of beautifully functional containers on an otherwise empty counter is more important than boring, unsexy data and time management. Organization is far more about the invisible, ongoing work than it is about the pretty stuff. Just like your career, one of your well-crafted performances once or twice a year is all the average fan will see of you, but what you grind out behind the scenes, daily, relentlessly, is what makes the stage magic possible.

With that clear, let's give some attention to organizing objects, starting with some concepts.

Space as a Resource

In Chapter 1, we talked about how time is a resource just like money. Now let's add a third form of currency: Space. Like time and money, physical space is a limited resource. Also like time and money, space is a somewhat interchangeable resource. Just as you can "buy" time with money, and you can lose money when you lose time, you can also literally buy more space with money, or sell extra space for money, and wasted space costs you both money and time. It's all connected.

For a touring musician, the skill of living in a small space is especially valuable because you have to fit your life into a few bags and gear cases on a regular basis. In reality, it's a valuable skill for any indie musician, whether you tour or not, because chances are you're not living in a mansion. With good object organization, you can live just fine in a normal house, or a basic apartment, or even a single rented room.

Arranging Your Stuff

You get to define how "organized" looks and functions when it comes to your own belongings and living space. As long as you have systems and they work for you, it doesn't matter whether they make sense or look nice to other people. You might have to make compromises in shared spaces, but you never have to obey some magazine cover.

Stuff-out and stuff-away:

We first looked at this concept in Chapter 2: Data. As you're organizing your space, keep in mind your visual preference of stuff out or stuff away and honor it as best you can. If you're a stuff-out with stuff-away housemates, the kitchen probably isn't going to be just the way you like it, but at least you can set up your bedroom to suit your needs. If you have to share a bathroom with someone of the opposite preference, agree to carve out a section that is yours alone (a drawer or shelf if you're a stuff-away, one side of the counter if you're a stuff-out), and then do your best to focus on your section and ignore the rest.

Like with like:

This is a classic organizational concept that helps in several ways: deciding where to put things, knowing where to look for them, and knowing when you need more or have too much. It means grouping things based on a similarity, such as what they're used for or where or when. Common examples in a home are bath towels together in the linen closet, spices in one drawer in the kitchen, or dog gear all on one shelf in the coat closet. In a band van, it makes sense to group things in the order you need to retrieve them. If you're loading in at the venue before checking in at the hotel, everybody's luggage goes in first, before all the gear: Last stuff in = first stuff out.

Modular systems:

This builds on like with like to make it easier for things to fit together in groupings. When you have items that you often take with you when you leave home, it makes sense for them to stay together all the time. Then you can easily take that portion of your stuff with you and put it away when you get home without rearranging everything. For example, in your clothes closet, hang all the clothes you can wear onstage together in one section so you don't have to look through everything to choose an outfit or pack for a tour. Keep the gear you use onstage or outside at rehearsal separate from what you only use at home. In your bathroom, keep all of the toiletries and tools that you use daily and also travel with together on the same shelf or in the same drawer, so when you pack you can simply grab everything from that space and know you've got what you need. When you return, everything gets plugged back into the space it came out of in one easy chunk.

Tricks for Decluttering

If you've got some clutter built up in your home, here are some concepts to help you get it down to a manageable level.

Contingencies:

Deciding where to start is often the hardest part of organizing your physical space. One way to figure out what will make a good starting point is to think about how organizing one area will affect, or be affected by, other areas. For example, if you want to organize a room that currently contains a bunch of stuff that needs to go to other rooms, will that stuff fit in the other rooms as they are, or do those rooms need to be organized first? If organizing your bedroom is contingent on organizing the basement, don't start with your bedroom—start with the basement. (Unless you don't mind dumping more stuff into the basement to be dealt with later. Not the best thing to do but it's a pretty common desperation move.)

Converting objects to data:

Our physical lives are becoming more streamlined with the ongoing digitization of information and tools. Right now, though, we're still in the transitional era of having belongings that could be digital but aren't. CDs, books, DVDs, printed photos, and paper documents are all examples. If you're really tight on space, look around for things you could convert to digital. Be warned that this will be difficult if you're especially sentimental or a tactile processor, but if you can digitize at least some of your music, photos, and documents, you'll free up some valuable space and be able to travel lighter through life.

Multi-use tools:

If you have a bottle opener, a corkscrew, and a pocketknife with a bottle opener and a corkscrew, you don't need the separate bottle opener and corkscrew. If you have a DVD player and a laptop that plays DVDs, you don't need the DVD player. (How long have you had that thing? Haha) You can keep them if you want to, but when you're looking for stuff to offload, weeding out redundant single-use items is an easy way to do it.

80/20 rule:

The Pareto Principle (introduced in Chapter 1) works amazingly well for sorting through belongings and deciding what to get rid of. When you start with the knowledge that you probably only wear one of every five of your t-shirts, weeding them out gets a lot easier.

Tactile sympathy:

Touching things makes you more likely to keep them. (Seriously. Science.) When you're trying to pare down your stuff, make decisions about items as you look at them, before you touch. You'll find it's easier to make rational choices. If you're at all sentimental, this will really help you to be more objective.

An oversimplified explanation of hoarding:

Keeping a lot of stuff does not make someone a "hoarder." I hate how media attention has gotten this so twisted. If your space is packed with stuff and you really, seriously cannot let go of it without causing yourself emotional distress, even though keeping it is also causing problems, don't let anyone force you to. Don't subject yourself to a "cleanout" like on those horrible TV shows. But do find a therapist who understands hoarding and can help you to let go of it at your own pace. True hoarding is a reaction to painful past experiences—things you might not even realize are related. It's not something to be ashamed of and it's also not something to just ignore or take lightly. Addressing it (gently, respectfully, and by your rules) will make your life so much happier.

•

Now you've got some guidance for dealing with your messy spaces, which I encourage you to do once you've got the more urgent time and data organizational jobs under control. Let's finish out this chapter with some good and bad habits, and then it's on to the last set of theories before we get into strategies.

Habits That Create Clutter

Acquisitiveness:

If you habitually acquire stuff—not necessarily useful or valuable stuff, just stuff you pick up on a whim—you're making life harder for yourself. Shopping as a hobby just generates clutter that you have to make room for and eventually get rid of. It's like overeating, gaining weight, and then having to work it off. Acquisitiveness can also be compulsive like overeating, so if you find that you have an actual problem with it, talk to a therapist and stop it before it gets even worse. But if you can curb it on your own, do so and replace it with a form of relaxation or amusement that won't be more trouble than it's worth.

Leaving hands-on projects unfinished:

This is especially common with tactile people, but it can happen to anyone. That pedalboard you started ... when are you going to get it working? That engine you tore down ... how long will it sit in pieces in the garage? What's keeping you from finishing that kegerator or costume or mural or yard sculpture? We can call these "exploratory projects"—things you started without a clear concept of how long they will take or whether you have everything you need to finish them. That's fine, but try not to have more than one of these going at a time.

Bad time management:

If you're always rushed, you're more likely to dump stuff in random spots all over your home and to trash your car and bag because you don't take the time to empty them out. The mail piles up to the point that you're not sure what's current and you don't want to get into it until you have time to really deal with it. You live with dirty laundry, dirty dishes, and overflowing trash cans, and you run out of stuff and then overreact and buy a ton of it because you don't take a second to put things on a shopping list as they're running low. Not judging ... I get it. If this is you, circle back to Chapter 1: Time.

Habits That Combat Clutter

Homes:

This is another concept we covered previously, in Chapter 2: Data. The basic idea is that you assign a home for everything you own. You don't always have to put everything away, but when you do want to put it away, you'll know where it goes because it has a home. Being able to slot stuff into a reserved space makes organizing your belongings so much easier. Once homes are established and you don't have to consciously think to remember what they are, you'll find it comes naturally to put stuff away: Why drop your keys just anywhere when there's a hook right by the door?

Meta-decisions:

This one should also be familiar from Chapter 2. Remember that "meta" means "about itself," so a meta-decision is a decision about deciding. It's a way of deciding about an entire category of stuff in advance, so you don't have to stop and think about it with each item. For example, suppose you've decided that when you get a physical CD, you will either rip it and pass it on, or just pass it on. Now whenever you get one, the only question is whether it's worth keeping the music digitally. Once you take the time to listen to it and rip it if you're going to, the physical item then goes to a friend or donation.

Constant organizing:

OK, not literally constant, but definitely ongoing. Tidying up as you go is a lot easier than doing it as a separate step, and it keeps your space at a more organized baseline all the time instead of only before company's coming.

Resale shopping:

Getting comfortable with this will help you to stop keeping too much stuff, in two ways. First, when you trust that you can find another plaid shirt or black skirt for a couple bucks at the local Goodwill, you won't feel compelled to keep 15 of them just in case. And second, you'll have an easy way to regularly resell or donate stuff that's just taking up space in your home.

CHAPTER 4:

THOUGHTS

So far we've talked about the three main categories of organization: your time, data, and belongings. Foundational to all of those is organizing your thoughts.

Don't panic. I'm not going to kill your creativity.

Often musicians, and artists in general, worry that focusing on systems and administrative processes will make their minds too structured to generate their art. They fear that organization will stifle their talent. It's a leap of faith to believe this, but actually, the exact opposite is true: Getting organized removes distractions and time-wasters that make it impossible to bliss out for hours in your creative zone. Musician Cody Cowan learned the payoff for getting organized when he became general manager of Austin's famed venue The Mohawk. "At first it seems like a drag," Cody recalled, "but then you find that systematizing the business side frees up time to step away when creative inspiration comes."

A baseline level of organized thinking is necessary for an organized existence, but you don't have to take it to the extreme. I don't expect or want my clients to try to become like me, constantly seeing patterns and systems everywhere, putting everything into checklists and spreadsheets. I want you to do the minimum necessary to get yourself the results you need, and I hope that means there will still be a lot of random cool stuff floating around in your mind.

Let's look at some concepts that will help you get your mental house decluttered enough to live in but not necessarily picture-perfect.

Focus and Distractions

Desire-focus is not the same as task-focus. We all know someone who's constantly posting about "got my eyes on the prize, working the plan, on that grind, 100% committed, #winning" but then shows up late for gigs and obviously hasn't rehearsed.

Maybe you've been that person. No judgment. I bring it up to make the point that not only do you have to act on your desire-focus, you also have to *know how* to act: How to set tasks and sustain attention well enough to do them. That's not something that just comes naturally to everyone. There's no shame if you don't know how: You can learn.

Distraction is what usually gets in the way of task-focus. It can come from boredom (the task is dull and you don't feel like doing it), from forgetting why it matters (you're not thinking about how it will move you toward your goal, so you don't feel like doing it), or from something going on in your physical or mental state (you're in pain, hungry, cold, tired, worried, sad, etc.).

Distractibility can keep you from starting on a task or it can pull you away from one before it's finished. So in order to control your task-focus (and fulfill your desire-focus), you have to be able to manage your level of distractibility.

The mechanism that mentally moves you from one activity to another is called switching. You can make it happen or you can just let it happen. If your plan was to work on song charts but you would rather watch vintage drumming videos so you keep going back to YouTube, you're allowing yourself to switch. If you consciously make yourself close YouTube and stick with the charting, you're forcing yourself to switch. When distractions intrude, your awareness of the intrusion and your ability to resist it with conscious switching is what will make the difference between productive vs. wasted time.

Switching is both an innate talent and a developed ability. Like music, some people are born with an aptitude for efficient switching, which makes it easier for them to hone their skill at it. Still, people who aren't naturally good switchers can develop some control over it—often to an impressive level, with enough practice.

Switching can happen quickly, like literally flipping a light switch, or it can happen gradually like a sunrise or sunset. The slower version tends to be easier to "force," but by definition it takes time. You probably already do it without realizing it.

Switching rituals:

People often have routines that put them into the right frame of mind for certain activities: behaviors done in basically the same order and often in the same place each time, like winding down for bed, warming up for exercise, or (a disturbing but scientifically valid example) preparing to use hard drugs. If you try to sleep before you're ready, especially if you're not in your own bed, you'll likely toss and turn awhile. If you spring into exercise without your usual warmup, you're at greater risk of injury. When drug users OD, it's often in an unfamiliar place like a hotel room.

The reason behind all of these scenarios is the interplay between your mind and your body as you prepare to do something. Your mind processes the environmental cues as you go through the behavioral ritual, and when it's finally time to do the thing, your body is as ready as it's able to be. If that preparatory ritual is disrupted, your ability to tolerate or do the thing correctly is impaired.

As the saying goes, people are creatures of habit. When you use this natural tendency with intention, it can make all the difference in your effectiveness. "I've always had morning routines, but now I'm getting really serious about it," says Austrian-born international touring artist Ulrich Ellison. "If you have a good morning routine, it can set you up for the whole day. There's so many things you can get sidetracked by ... at the end of the day you have a feeling you didn't really accomplish anything." Ulrich's morning routine includes "a little bit of a physical workout, and then some guitar playing, about 20 minutes in the zone, where nothing distracts me. If I can do that every morning, then whatever the day will bring, I got the most important part done."

Fast switching:

Easing yourself into the next thing with a gradual switch is great when you can do it, but in reality, we often don't have the time. Can you afford to spend half an hour getting used to the idea that you're going to do a social media post? Probably not. Yet as much as we need to, fast switching can be difficult to do on demand. Even worse, it can be hard to prevent when we don't want it (distractions) and there are plenty of times when it will be imposed on us against our will (interruptions). So the best you can hope for with fast switching is to have some control over it.

Multitasking is a form of fast switching. Your mind can't actually do two different things at once; the best it can do is toggle between them quickly. If your switching frequency outpaces your ability to fully process what you're doing on each task, you'll do a substandard job because you're not giving either one your complete attention. When you become skilled enough to sing and play piano or guitar at the same time (and do it well), it's no longer multitasking—your mind has melded them into a single activity.

Hyperfocus is your reward when you succeed in ignoring distractions and locking the switch into place for the time being. This is what's happening when you're "in the zone," as Ulrich Ellison said above. This mental state is the best for deep, complex, creative thought. Unfortunately, hyperfocus often ends unpleasantly, with a startling interruption, or it dissolves as you run out of ideas or mental energy. But hey, it's great while it lasts. If you practice getting into this state quickly and frequently, it will become a skill that serves you very well, in both your admin tasks and your creative endeavors.

Macro/Micro Focus

Being able to give regular attention to both the big picture and the daily details is one of the greatest challenges, and one of the most valuable outcomes, of being organized. As a one-person operation, it's easy to default to firefighting mode: Dealing with the present as it happens and setting aside future planning out of sheer exhaustion and overwhelm. Figuring out how to get ahead of that is what elevates you to the next level.

Ed Hamell, the one-man acoustic punk band known as Hamell on Trial, is well-versed in the challenges that come with being a self-managed solo act and a full-time dad. "The good thing about having a kid is, you know where the priority lies," says Ed. "It's the kid. Keeping a roof over his head, spending time together. The priority isn't being a rock star. Then the next priority is the integrity of the work." In over 20 years of prolific recording and relentless touring, he's developed impressive efficiency and productivity, but the long-range advance activities remain daunting.

Responding to my admiration of the systems he's developed for touring nationwide by car, Ed reflected, "I do feel like I'm organized, but there are some qualifications." Despite having become pro-level at social media (with a huge assist from his teenage son, Detroit, who tours with him on summer breaks), comprehensive advance promotion of future shows is out of reach for this one-man army: "I wish I was playing to bigger crowds, and I think if I had more time to plan and organize, and I didn't have to worry about the immediate bills, the rent, the car payment, whatnot, then I could work it so you book the room, you promote like crazy, you do it six months in advance, and you get 300-400 people. But I don't have that luxury. But in terms of my day-to-day thing, I think I do pretty darn well."

The most important form of switching:

Simultaneous macro and micro focus is intertwined with everything we've talked about so far—organizing your time, data, belongings, and thoughts—and it applies to every aspect of your music career. Focusing only on the present accomplishes today's tasks, but it doesn't inform what tomorrow's tasks should be. Focusing only on the future is simply dreaming without doing. Continuously thinking future-and-present, present-and-future is a switching skill that you absolutely must have if you want to build a career according to your own specifications.

The frequency of this switch is up to you. In corporate jargon, we're talking about how often you step back from your daily deliverables to focus on strategic planning. (I know, a lot of this jargon deserves the mockery it gets, but there are some valid concepts buried in the buzzwords.) When things are going well, you might only need strategic planning once a quarter. When things are tough, you'll need it more frequently. Some people revisit the plan daily. We'll get into more detail about this in Chapter 5: Direction.

Chronic Disorganization

Most people find it difficult to stay focused and organized at least once in a while. But if it's been a lifelong, daunting challenge for you, there could be something more to it. Chronic disorganization is the term for when you've been disorganized most or all of your life, it causes you problems pretty much every day, and there's nothing coming in the future that's going to fix it. (The opposite, situational disorganization, is temporary; when the situation resolves, you go back to your normal functional state.)

Attention deficit/hyperactivity disorder, or AD/HD, is a common cause of chronic disorganization, but there are others including chronic physical pain or fatigue, head injuries (even old ones), or substance abuse.

Chronic disorganization is not a character flaw. It's not laziness or lack of ambition. Some chronically disorganized people find that hard to believe, since they've spent their lives being ashamed of it and blaming themselves, but it truly is just a problem to be solved. No doubt, it's harder for a CD person to get organized—often it takes one-on-one coaching plus professional help for any underlying mental or physical causes—but it certainly can be done.

Mood Interference

Even if you're not chronically disorganized, emotional distress can demolish your best-laid plans and systems. Both depression and anxiety make it difficult and sometimes impossible to concentrate. The intrusive thoughts that accompany these conditions can crowd out all productive thought and send you looking for some sort of escape. Often that escape is something unhealthy, but even if it's not, it's still keeping you from making progress on your goals.

Everyone has periods of sadness or worry; that's not clinical depression or anxiety. If the mood doesn't lift on its own in a few days, and especially if it can't be attributed to a specific cause like a breakup or the death of a loved one, it's time for professional help. You wouldn't ignore persistent hoarseness in your voice or a tremor in your hands, so don't ignore a neurochemical disruption either.

Your Needs Are Out of Order

Even if you're blessed with good concentration and no chronic disorganization or emotional upheaval, there is one burden that you're almost certainly carrying as an indie musician.

You might have heard of Maslow's Hierarchy of Needs. Abraham Maslow was a psychologist who developed the theory that every human has the same basic needs, and that those needs must be fulfilled in the same order. First is physiological needs including food, water, and sleep. Once those are satisfied, a person needs security: physical safety, shelter, money, health. After you get safe and secure, you need love and belonging: enriching relationships of all sorts. Get all of that handled and you can move on to esteem: accomplishment, respect. And with all of those needs met, you can finally work on what Maslow called self-actualization: Achieving your dreams, your goals, your full potential.

Of course you're doing it totally out of order. You're trying to accomplish your creative goals—to self-actualize as a successful musician—long before all of your other needs have been met.

Hey, I support that. Plenty of artists have done exactly that, so why not you? In fact, you pretty much have to. Your innate talent doesn't automatically translate into ability: It must be continually developed through ongoing learning and practice, and you can't simply put off that development until it's convenient. Besides, if you waited until you were totally safe, secure, loved, and respected before you started making music, what you produced would probably be soulless and boring, if you ever got around to it at all.

So you've got to work on your music well before you hit self-actualization. Just understand that this is one of the reasons it's such an uphill climb. Put some energy toward those more basic needs to at least keep them from interfering with your ability to stay organized and focused on your music. That might be as close as you can get to "life balance" for now.

●

All of the concepts from these first four chapters are woven throughout the rest of the book. Come back to this section when you need to get reoriented to the fundamentals. In the next section, we're starting on strategic thinking. The first objective there is to get crystal clear about your values and goals. That is the only way to make informed choices about how best to steer your indie music career.

Let's end this chapter with some thoughts on cognitive clutter.

Habits That Clutter Your Thoughts

Awfulizing:

Also called catastrophizing. It's a form of worrying, but instead of just a general uneasiness about something, this is imagining the worst possible outcome and letting yourself dwell on that possibility, perhaps even replaying the imagined disaster over and over in your mind. Some people call this "praying for what you don't want." You might not be able to prevent the initial thought of the bad thing that could happen, but you can train yourself out of the habit of lingering on it. One way is to force yourself to imagine and mentally act out the best possible outcome instead.

Mind-reading:

This is similar to awfulizing because when we do it, it's not usually in a positive way. Mind-reading means expending energy imagining what another person thinks, even playing out conversations and scenes in your head and causing yourself the same emotional reaction as if those scenes had actually happened. Don't torture yourself like this. If you really need to know what a person is thinking, ask. Wondering is not worth the stress.

Too much newness:

Some days can seem like you're being bombarded with a meteor shower of new ideas, and you want to explore them all. You'll do better to record them (audio or in writing) just enough to capture the concept and then return to focusing on the tasks you need to complete or to the creative work you were already doing, and come back to those new ideas later. If you're already close to capacity with the ideas you currently have, avoid your usual sources of new ideas until you've digested the ones in progress.

Drama:

If you want to know whether you have too much drama in your life, see what happens when you check out for a day to concentrate. Is your phone blowing up with friends or family who need something or who are mad that you're not answering right away? What does your personal social media look like: Mostly people bitching or reporting sad news? If your interactions with people are mostly about them and their needs, anger, and sadness (even if you kind of enjoy those soap operas), think about what a drain that is on your daily energy.

Panicking about backsliding:

You will have setbacks—everybody does. They don't mean all is lost. In the context of organization, backsliding might look like 200 unopened emails, or having no merch t-shirts for this weekend's shows because you forgot to reorder, or some messages to your Facebook page that you should have answered the day they came in and now they just make you cringe. This is a great time for that Nike slogan: Just do it. It will be easier to catch back up than it was to create and establish the system in the first place, so just do it and keep moving.

Habits That Clarify Your Thoughts

Sleep:

Sleep deprivation is the best way to make yourself temporarily stupid. If you're sitting at your computer at 4 a.m. with your eyes crossing and you're making no sense in that email you're trying to write, just stop. Go to sleep. It will be easier when you wake up.

Movement:

It doesn't have to be full-on exercise if you're not into that. Just getting up and wandering around for a bit can help to clear the cobwebs and shake loose some new ideas. If you are into exercise, though, and especially if you've found that it makes a difference in your energy and happiness, then go do it. Like sleep, sometimes the best time for it is when you think you don't have the time.

Reviewing your written values and goals:

This can get you reoriented when you've got a lot on your mind and you're struggling to focus on some mundane administrative task, or when you're feeling discouraged. Even if the goals seem out of reach today, the values will remind you of what's most important to you.

Reviewing past similar work:

Use that procedures manual I suggested in Chapter 1 to recall how you did something before so you don't have to figure it out again. Use past emails and press releases as templates for new ones. If you're stuck on what to say in social media posts, scroll back through the last several dozen that you did. Look at them in the platform where you posted them so you see them in their final format, or look at the unformatted text in your planning document or spreadsheet—whichever works better for you.

Phone games (sometimes):

Yes, they can be a time waster, but a few rounds now and then can also cleanse your mental palate. Go for the ones that have short, clearly delineated rounds or levels, like solitaire, mah jongg, a crossword puzzle, or good ol' Candy Crush. Bonus: Tetris will hone your skills in packing the band van. ;)

Noodling (maybe):

If what you're trying to clarify has to do with music, this might or might not help. Don't do it if you're already stuck and frustrated with that instrument; try a different instrument or just stop playing and go do something else for a bit. But if you need a breakthrough with your business tasks, or just a break from them, a bit of noodling may be the perfect thing.

Checking in with trusted advisors:

Who do you chat with when you need to sort out a problem, get a new idea, or be reminded of why you're doing all of this? Sometimes these are people who have a knack for cutting to the heart of the issue, offering succinct insight, and/or putting you and your bullshit in check. Other times, these are people who pull you out of your stuck headspace with funny stories or a shared activity and remind you, simply with their presence, that they love and support you. And then there are those people who remind you of the life you don't want and give you fresh motivation to keep pushing. They all help, in their way.

SECTION 2: STRATEGIC CHOICES

Every career is loaded with choices, but self-employment is even more so. I would argue that self-employment is less risky than having a boss because you have more freedom of choice, but with that freedom comes more risk of choices that take you far down the wrong path before you realize you're lost.

Some forms of self-employment have outcomes that are relatively easy to anticipate, which makes them lower-risk: If you open a Whataburger franchise, you know what you'll be selling and you know there will be people to buy it. Many strategic choices have already been made for you—especially the ones that would expose you to particularly high risk.

In contrast, there is very little you can predict or anticipate about the outcomes of self-employment as a musician. Franchise owners get a franchisee manual that walks them through how to run the restaurant and how to know whether they're succeeding. It's nowhere near that cut and dried for you as an indie musician. You have dozens of paths to choose from under the umbrella of "music career," so you're faced with thousands of options and hundreds of choices right from the start, and you're continually confronted with more choices as you go. With so many options, every decision you make is strategic, and every strategic decision is far more important than you might realize.

I'm not going to tell you what to choose. There are plenty of other music-biz books and blogs that do that. Instead, I'm helping you to organize your thinking so you can make informed choices. This section starts with a chapter on choosing and mapping out your direction, then continues with chapters on refining your strategy in various areas of operation that all contribute to your overall direction. Some of these areas are heavy with organizational challenges (promotion is a big one) and others have relatively fewer administrative pitfalls which makes them relatively easier to organize.

There will probably be aspects of your career that aren't specifically addressed in these chapters and questions you have that aren't answered here. This is when you'll start applying what you've learned through your studious attention to organizational theory. When you can solve your own problem by identifying the relevant theories and choosing or building the right system to address it, you will have graduated from getting organized to being organized.

Perspective reminder: As a professional musician, you've got talent and ability that most people don't have and couldn't develop even with great effort. In contrast, what we're talking about in this book is much more universally achievable. Don't be intimidated at the idea of custom-building your own organizational framework. You've already accomplished something much more difficult.

CHAPTER 5:

DIRECTION

Committing to a career in music is a pivotal step. It's a lot like deciding to build yourself a house. You probably have a vague idea of what you want it to look like, where you want to build it, and how big you want it to be, but you have a lot of design work to do to bring it into existence.

This chapter will get you thinking about the direction you want your music career to take, so that you can start to flesh out the initial design and begin construction. Continuing the house-building analogy, if you're already a professional musician, you can use this chapter to remodel the career you already have if needed. We'll begin with some pertinent concepts to help you take an organized approach to this process and then start framing the structure upwards from your foundational values.

Informed Choice

You might have heard this phrase in a healthcare context. Whenever you have a medical procedure, or if you see a mental health professional, the provider is legally and ethically required to obtain your "informed consent" for treatment. To do so, they must give you the answers to all of your questions, and not only that, they must also anticipate questions you haven't asked and give you those answers too. When that has been done, your consent is considered an informed choice.

You can and should aim to make informed choices in all of your business planning and decision-making, through careful research and consultation with your peers and trusted advisors. That might sound obvious, but when you put these words on it and make it a conscious intention, you're much less likely to be surprised by outcomes or to get stuck with an unwanted precedent because you didn't think through the decision carefully enough.

Precedent

With any system you create, you're setting a precedent for how things will be done going forward. This is good when you're doing it intentionally and in an informed manner, but if a decision is made hastily or without context, you set yourself up to have to do things the same way in the future even if you can't or don't want to keep it up.

Bad precedents get set inadvertently when you don't realize that you are in fact establishing a system. If you hear from someone else or find yourself saying, "That was just for that one time. I didn't mean it would be that way forever," you're seeing the fallout of a negative or unintentional precedent.

Sustainability

Designing sustainable systems is critical to staying organized. I don't mean sustainable in the recycle-not-trash sense of the word (although that's great too if it's your jam). In organizing, sustainable means that the system does not require more resources—time, money, energy, interest—than you can consistently afford to give. Sustainability is a key consideration along with precedent. Taken together, the wisdom of precedent and sustainability is, "Don't start something you can't finish."

Contingencies

I introduced this idea in Chapter 3 as it applies to organizing physical spaces. Now let's look at it in the context of strategic planning.

Sometimes when you want to do one thing, you have to do something else first. Accomplishing one is contingent on accomplishing the other. And usually there are more than two levels of contingency. If you want to try for radio play, you have to make a recording, which means you need access to a studio and recording professionals, which probably means you need some money. If you want to go on tour, you have to book some road shows, and to do that you need videos for remote talent buyers to evaluate, and to get those you need to play some local shows and get someone to record them. These examples are multi-layered and yet they're still oversimplified.

Being able to strategize backwards through the contingencies from the end goal to the first step is a crucial component of organized planning.

Autonomous Systems

While it's essential for you to be able to recognize contingencies in your goal steps, it's also valuable to learn how to avoid building too many of them into your systems. If a plan or strategy or system is dependent on the success of one or more other systems—particularly systems outside of your control, like those belonging to a venue—then it's vulnerable to failing just when you need it most.

Here are some contingencies that you'd better make sure are worth it: If you want to use in-ear monitors instead of the standard wedges, you need to take extra care to coordinate with the venue's sound engineer. If you did ticket presales for a live-streamed show, you need to make sure you can get online at the appointed time. If you want to tour internationally and take the whole band instead of using subs in each destination city, your process for hiring bandmembers needs to include a criminal background check.

If your stage sound didn't depend on your own delicate gear and your setup wasn't burdened by an additional tech vulnerability and your tour didn't hang on your guitarist's felony record, your systems would be more autonomous. A large part of being organized is planning ahead to prevent problematic contingencies and to minimize the risk when they can't be avoided.

Diminishing and Delayed Returns

When the payoff on an action slows down, you're receiving "diminishing returns" on your effort. At that point, you need to ask yourself whether it's worth continuing. Is the last flavorless bit of that slushie worth the exertion and the grating slurping noises it will take to get it? When the initial rush at the merch table is over, is it worth delaying your three-hour drive home any longer for the possibility of a couple more CD sales? You'll be called upon regularly to make decisions on diminishing returns, and you'll get better at them as you gain experience in the industry. Ensuring you have the data you need to make informed choices (analytics about social media campaigns, demographic data about your fanbase, sales figures for comparison in your markets and genre, capacity and average attendance at your upcoming venues, etc.) will also help a lot.

A different but related concept is delayed returns. This is even harder to gauge because instead of watching good results slow down, you're waiting for an initial effort to start working. Here you're vulnerable to the "gambler's fallacy"—the belief that the longer you keep doing a particular thing, the more likely it is to pay off. Yet on the other hand, we all know that persistence is the key to success at anything. So how do you decide when to call it quits on a strategy or campaign?

The difference is … ready for this? … contingencies again. If the actions of your effort are entirely independent of one another, believing that effort will pay off eventually is the gambler's fallacy. But if your effort is proceeding in steps that are dependent on other steps, then the odds truly are changing.

If you send a booking pitch to 10 out-of-town venues that have probably never heard of you, and then do it the exact same way with 10 other venues, and 10 other venues, you might think that you're more likely to get a booking with each round, but you're not. The 3rd or 5th or 10th roll of those dice is no more likely to pay off than the first: Since nothing has changed with your process, the odds are the same with each roll. However, if you send that pitch to the first 10, follow up with reasonable persistence, finally get several "no"s but make changes to the pitch based on any feedback you receive or new ideas you have, and then send the revised pitch to 10 more and keep repeating that cycle, you do indeed increase your odds with each round, because you have changed the process each time. If you know you're doing it better and better, delayed returns become worth waiting for.

●

That's it for initial concepts on direction. Let's move into foundation-building.

Identify Your Values

It's a given that making music is one of your life values. What else? What other elements must you have in order to be happy? These might be types of relationships, specific activities or habits, certain physical or emotional states, particular circumstances, or something else.

I'm not going to give you a list to choose from, and please don't ask Google for one. This isn't about listing virtuous character traits that you think you should have. That doesn't tell you what you actually value. In fact, it would be more useful to think about times when you've been on your worst behavior and regretted it. What didn't you like about yourself in those moments? In other words, which of your values were you violating? Again, don't jump to what society would say you should regret. You're having this conversation with yourself alone, so be honest.

Maybe you've done some things others would condemn but you're not a bit sorry. Look at those times too and pluck out the values that you were exercising in those situations. It's often under duress that we discover what our true values are. Think of times you've been tested and what they taught you about what's truly important to you.

If you're thinking this is flaky and unnecessary and you just want to get organized so you can survive in this business, hold up. This is part of getting organized. There are some careers where being fraudulent with yourself can work—mostly the ones that pay very well. It's easier to compromise your values when you're making a ton of money in the process. A $400,000-per-year surgeon who loves her work and also regrets missing her kids' childhood for it can justify her values conflict with the assertion that she's doing it to provide them with the best education and extracurricular opportunities. A $40,000-per-year musician can't make that same rationalization. As a self-employed artist, more than most people, your career must be fully aligned with your values.

Name Your Long-Term Goals

"Make my living with my music" is not a goal. It's a values-based aspiration, which is a good start, but it's not specific enough to be a goal. In order to build your house, you need to know how you want the rooms to look and function. You have a million options but you don't have the resources to pursue every one of them, so you have to choose a handful to focus on.

Who are your role models? Do you know someone who has the type of music career you want? Perhaps not, and that can make your goal-setting more difficult. The most visible musicians are famous and assumed to be raking in tons of money, which doesn't make it easy to see that you can earn a comfortable living as a professional musician and be far from famous, not on the radio, and not headlining or even playing the huge festivals.

If you don't live in a town where live music is prevalent, it might be easier to spot and learn from successfully self-employed people in other fields. We'll talk about how you can meet them in the Networking section of Chapter 7. Most successfully self-employed people own businesses that no one's ever heard of outside of their town. They might want to be respected or even famous within their own industry, but they don't care about being a household name. (That's a curse unique to entertainment.) As an indie musician, your business will look a lot more like those folks' than like a label artist's.

Independent music career goals might include:

- Make enough money from music to cover all of my bills
- Become a regular on the festival circuit
- Assemble and lead my own band
- Get radio play
- Teach music lessons online
- Build a solo career
- Become a household name
- Win a Grammy
- Join a solid band in need of a great new [what you play]
- Tour with [your hero act]
- Start an indie label
- Earn six figures a year and have a house on the lake
- Have a residency at [a hometown club]
- Have a family and home life along with my music career
- Record with [your hero producer]
- Open my own recording studio
- Make [$####] per year from sync licensing placements
- Get a label deal
- Release [#] new songs per year

These are just examples of some people's goals. You probably have some that aren't listed here. Yours might even be the opposite of some of these. Maybe you don't care about radio and loathe the very idea of major labels. Maybe you think a local residency is minor and you want to be hugely famous. Fine. Rejecting others' goals is a valid way to identify your own. Take some time to write yours down. You'll be revisiting them regularly.

Identify Short-Term Goals

Articulating interim goals for each long-term goal is a solid way to measure your progress. Daniel Eyes, frontman of Daniel Eyes & The Vibes, applies a straightforward sensibility to his career trajectory. "Create goals that have shorter expiration dates on them that you can use as stepping stones to that long-term goal," says Daniel. "Those short-term goals help me to be able to see if I'm making progress. If my progress seems to stagnate, then I know I need to change those short-term plans. The long-term plan might not necessarily need to change itself." When things seem to be going astray, this approach helps Daniel to lock into a new strategy: "You can't get caught up in what went wrong for too long," he says. "Once you have an idea, try it but make sure it's an organized effort."

Choose Your Lines of Business

Which of these roles will you take on as part of your music career? This is similar to a college student choosing a major, except that you will likely have 4 or 5 or more of these that together define your "job":

Local live performer	Band owner	Recording producer
Touring musician	Bandmember	DJ
Tribute/cover artist	Session musician	Live sound engineer
YouTube performer	Sub/guest/"side" player	Live show producer
Songwriter	Music instructor	Indie label owner
Recording artist	Custom instrument builder	Recording studio owner
Sync-licensed musician	Recording engineer	Musician peer consultant

In business-owner lingo, these are referred to as "revenue streams" or "lines of business." Each is like a department within your company. That might be hard to picture since you're the one doing all of the jobs, but that's the way it goes for self-employed people: We wear all the hats. And in addition to all of these skill-delivery roles, you will also have the role of administrator for each of them (at least until you're able to hire some help).

Some of your roles will be the most active and others will be infrequent. Some will be the most labor-intensive while others are relatively easy money.

Look at your goals list and your chosen lines of business. There should be a lot of overlap: You'll need a line of business to carry out each goal, and at least one goal to set the course for each line of business.

One choice about lines of business that leads us into the next chapter is whether you want to have a solo career or be the leader or a member of a band. You don't necessarily have to be an actual one-person band to go the solo route. Some solo artists always perform alone, but others have a roster of side players that they hire as needed, and still others have a regular backing band but remain the focal point and the billed name of all of their shows and recordings.

By the same token, there are different ways to "be a band." When you're starting a band, there are various ways to organize its leadership (and if you're joining one, you need to know how it's structured). A band with a distinctive frontperson is different from a solo artist with a backing band, although to audiences they generally look the same. A band led by the drummer will be assumed to be run by the singer unless the drummer happens to sing lead. That's just how audiences think, as you probably already realize, and for your marketing purposes it doesn't really matter that they know who's in charge. But here, behind the scenes, you should sort out those differences clearly from the beginning to avoid unnecessary confusion and reorganization down the road.

Consider the Cost

This brings in elements of sustainability and contingencies as we discussed above. An indie music career, like every other small business, has associated expenses. Ignoring that—failing to budget, throwing money at random ideas, and finding yourself unable to sustain whatever momentum you do generate—is a common mistake among start-up bands. Veteran musician and music business consultant Alex Vallejo sees that rock & roll gleam in the eyes of artists just starting out who want a manager, a booking agent, a PR rep, a web designer, a social media manager, a band van, and more. It's great to dream big and set enormous goals, he says, but his job is to help artists calibrate those dreams with reality: "I tell them, 'Let's look at the attainable and realistic. What are realistic things you can do right now?' Most bands don't have any money but they make a list of what they want and I'm like, that list is about $20,000-$30,000. So let's make the free list—what's affordable, what's available to you, what realistically can you do with where you're at right now."

Thoughts to Ponder on Direction

Starting direction and ongoing navigation:

The theories at the beginning of this chapter apply as you're setting your initial direction and as you're steering your course over the years. Your direction might change over time, but you want those changes to occur because you intentionally changed your navigation, not because you got lost. Starting out with a well-considered and well-documented plan will help you to remember where you intended to go.

Projects accomplish goals:

Goals are fulfilled by completing projects. If you think of your career as one enormous project, with your lines of business as sub-projects, you can then zoom in far enough to see which of those sub-projects will bring which of your goals to fruition.

Projects differ from goals in that they are fully within your control. "Win a Grammy" is not a project—it's a goal. "Submit for Grammy consideration" is a project which you might undertake within your role of songwriter, recording artist, session musician, or recording engineer or producer.

No final destination:

Speaking metaphorically, some say you can't have a clear direction without a clear destination. I don't think that is an ideal metaphor for a music career. Destination implies arriving and stopping. That's probably not what you're trying to do. Instead of thinking of this as a path to a single end point, think of it as a path to a region you want to keep traveling around within.

Behave like the business owner you are:

Professionalism will distinguish you from the crowd. "Definitely, you need to think of yourself as a business," says Rakefet Laviolette, booking agent for the award-winning world music band Rattletree and co-owner of the Rattletree School of Marimba. "It's how you present yourself and that confidence you bring with you. Bookers work with us because of the music, yes, but also because we're easy to work with. We have our contracts in order, we follow up, we do our promo. I mean, if you're just kind of dabbling in it and it's fun and it's a side project, great, but if you're making your living through it, or you want to, you really need to take it seriously because there are many other people who do. You need to rise to that level. Take it seriously and be known for being the best and being reliable."

CHAPTER 6:

BUSINESS STRUCTURE & FINANCES

If you've read from the beginning of the book, you've gotten far enough into your goal-setting to define policies about the financial and legal aspects of your music business.

First and always, remember this: Whether you're a solo artist, bandleader, or bandmember, you are a self-employed individual. If you don't establish this from the beginning, you might get a nasty dose of income tax reality, or find yourself entangled in an ugly breakup that leaves you with no business identity apart from your now-former band, or any number of other unpleasant surprises that can be avoided by understanding the implications of self-employment.

Establish Your Self-Employed Status

In the U.S., you have two basic projects to complete when you become self-employed: Create your business as a legal entity (sole proprietor, LLC, etc.) and acquire a Federal Tax Identification Number, a.k.a. an Employer Identification Number or EIN. This is true whether you start a band, join one, or remain strictly a solo or contract player, and regardless of whether you have a day job which withholds income tax from your paycheck. In fact, if you are getting paid in any way other than a paycheck with taxes withheld, you are already self-employed and responsible for knowing what you're supposed to be doing differently with your taxes. You might have some catching up to do.

If you join a band, on the music side you're coming in as their amazing new percussionist or bassist etc., but on the business side, you're joining as either a contracted player or as a member of their existing business. You will want to understand the legal and financial ins and outs of these scenarios well in advance.

If you start a band, you might be the sole owner and pay your players as employees or contractors, or you might choose to form a partnership which gives part ownership of the band to one or more others who may or may not be musicians.

All of these situations have tax implications, which means you would be wise to get advice from a finance professional before you make decisions that could have unanticipated consequences. U.S. taxpayers can consult the IRS website at www.IRS.gov for an introduction to the process of becoming self-employed, starting your own business, or entering into a partnership. You can also get free—yes, free—business mentoring through the Small Business Administration (www.SBA.gov) which connects you with advisors to help you understand your options and get things set up correctly from the start.

Separate Your Business Finances

One of your most important organizational tasks as a self-employed person is keeping your business and personal finances separate. It can take some getting used to and will probably seem inconvenient and unnecessarily redundant at first, but being sloppy with this can get you into seriously hot water with the IRS. The easiest way to separate them is to have two checking accounts—one business, one personal—and use the business one exclusively for business (all self-employment income and expenses) and the personal one exclusively for non-business.

Once you have your business name registered and a business bank account set up, give payers your tax ID instead of your Social Security number and have payments written to your business, not to your personal name. If you are also still receiving pay as a regular employee (W-2 income, with taxes taken out), those payments should continue to be made to your personal name and SSN and deposited into your personal account.

You will need to learn what constitutes a business expense. Again, study the IRS website for these rules and follow your accountant's advice. There are specific instructions on how to know what counts as a valid business expense and what does not. Eventually you'll have this stuff memorized and you won't have to stop and think about which card to use at the checkout.

If you co-own your band, it will need its own checking account in addition to your own personal and business accounts. This is because the band income is not yours alone. The band will pay you, the other owner(s), and anyone else it employs or contracts with. Unless you're already experienced with running a small business, I strongly recommend you get an accountant's help with this scenario.

Managing an extra bank account:

When you have more than one checking account and not a ton of money, it's tricky to keep the right amount in each. If your bank will allow it (not all do), activate the option to transfer online from your business account to your personal account and vice-versa. This makes it so much easier to quickly transfer money (i.e. making an "owner draw" from biz to personal or "owner loan" from personal to biz) if one account is low or overdrawn. If you can't do it online, at least make sure you will be able to make transfers by phone.

If you have autodebits coming out of either or both accounts, calculate the most that will be debited from each account within any 7-day span. (That timeframe allows for variances in withdrawals that are supposed to happen on the same date each month but don't.) Then, in your online banking portal, nickname each account with the minimum balance you need to keep in it at any given time to cover those autodebits (e.g. "Pers ck—keep $300")

Who Owns This Band?

If you're joining an existing band, you'll want to know some details about how the band is run. Be careful here: You don't want to come across as overly nosy, a control freak looking to take over, or a detached hired gun who expects to be compensated for every little thing. Still, this is information you need, so figure out how to diplomatically ask these questions.

If you're the band owner, consider how you will answer these questions from prospective members. If you haven't yet decided some of these points, now is the time to set your policies. You might want to handle some of these situations differently depending on the circumstances, and that's fine. But think it through now so you're not pressured to make a snap decision later.

- *Who are the official owners of this band? Is anyone else involved in the band's legal or financial decisions?* The rest of the band might be consulted on some or all decisions, or on none. There might also be an attorney, accountant, manager, or other outside advisor who has influence on these decisions. Notice that this is separate from the question of who makes the band's creative and/or strategic decisions.
- *How is my pay decided?* Are you contracting for a flat rate per gig or a percentage? If your pay will vary by event, you might also want to know who makes the booking decisions and what they consider a minimum acceptable payment for the band.
- *What expenses will be reimbursed?* You will incur expenses, even for local performances. Are bandmembers reimbursed for parking, tolls, gas? If you're expected to dress a certain way, do you receive a wardrobe allowance? On the road, are you covered for meals, laundry, lodging, out-of-network cellular minutes/data? When going out of town, is van rental or airfare covered, or do players drive their personal vehicles?
- *Will I be included in songwriting or recording? If so, will I be paid by the hour, by the song, or with points?* Depending on where the band is in its development, they might not have answers to these questions yet. It's OK to wait and see, if you're comfortable with that. It would also be completely reasonable for them to want to get some experience with you before deciding whether you'll be a good fit in the studio, so even with an established band, the answer might be, "We'll see."
- *What are bandmembers' typical unpaid time commitments?* In other words, will you be expected to do anything for free? Chances are you will, and this is not necessarily bad—you just need to know so you can make an informed decision. This could include anything from rehearsals, media appearances, and unpaid gigs to time spent putting up posters, participating in the band's social media or crowdfunding campaigns, or making music videos.
- *Will I be expected to chip in for expenses not covered by band revenue?* This could include rehearsal space rental, paid promotion, purchase of merch for resale, festival application fees, or any of the expenses of touring or recording. If you are expected to contribute to these, is it a loan or an expenditure that you won't get back dollar for dollar? (If it is to be an unreimbursed expenditure, remember to write it off as a business expense for yourself.)
- *What happens to the merch money and tips?* This one can be a fight-starter if it's not established from the beginning. Some bands put the money from the tip jar and merch sales back into a band fund; others divvy it up among the players. There is no single right way to do it, but one thing is certain: If a bandmember gets a lousy $20 for the performance but sees brisk sales at the merch table and doesn't know where that money is going, resentment will ensue.

Choose Your Moneymakers

Continuing our consideration of goals and lines of business from the last chapter, how are you planning to bring home the bacon? Gigging might be the first way you think of that musicians make money, but there are others to consider. Each one will add to your administrative workload, so be sure the revenue will actually be worth the effort.

Physical recordings and other merch:

Digital music sales can be set for automatic order fulfillment, so those won't require admin time other than the initial distribution setup and monitoring. CDs can also be sold as "print on demand," which also means automatic order fulfillment. But selling CDs, vinyl, t-shirts, and other swag at your shows and taking orders through your website which you then have to ship are both labor-intensive endeavors. Do you have the human resources to do these jobs and still make a profit on the sales?

Keeping an inventory of merch requires upfront payment to buy the stock, space to store it, and time to organize and maintain it, in addition to the costs of selling at shows and shipping mail orders. Are you able to invest $500-$1,000 or more at a time to keep your merch stocked?

There is a compelling argument that merch isn't just about sales—it's also an essential form of marketing. Does this hold true for you, even if the direct revenue from it is very low?

Streaming:

We've all heard that having your music available to stream on Spotify, Pandora, Google Play, Apple Music, and other platforms pays next to nothing, but have you looked into it and done your own research? Similar to merch, is it an essential form of marketing? Is it unprofitable at worst, or are there actual drawbacks to doing it?

Sync licensing:

There is a lot to read and understand about sync licensing, but basically it means allowing your music to be used in others' projects in exchange for some type of compensation. It's a hot field right now and some artists are making a lot of money with it. If you want to go after sync deals on your own, are you sure you can respond in the short timeframe needed to secure them? Are you well-versed enough in the contract particulars to make a quick decision about each offer? Or would it be more realistic to find a representative you trust to make the approvals and contract decisions for you in exchange for a cut of the payment? Whether or not you use a middleman, you will need to have your music organized more precisely than you otherwise might. Chapter 14 has a sample Sync Licensing Tracker for this.

Monetized videos:

Do you have videos on YouTube or plan to? Have you looked into options for allowing advertising around or within your videos in exchange for payment? If you don't already have regular video production as a component of your career, would it be worthwhile to make it a priority or would it detract from effort better spent on another aspect of your business?

Contracts and Other Pitfalls

It's dangerous to sign a business contract without having an attorney review it. Even if you can understand what it says (with or without heavy assistance from Google), the risky part isn't so much what's in it. The biggest risk lies in what's left out. A music business attorney will point out anything in the contract that is not in your best interests, but even more important, s/he will suggest verbiage that should be added, either to clarify potential gray areas that might not be obvious in the existing wording or to address situations that aren't mentioned at all.

For example, suppose you receive an offer for a great-paying corporate event at a local park. The contract looks straightforward to you, so you sign and return it. You arrive on time and soundcheck, but before you can start, a massive thunderstorm rolls in and forces the show to be cancelled. While the rest of the band scrambles to get the gear out of the rain, you track down the event producer to collect your payment and he tells you that you won't be paid because you didn't perform. Only then do you realize that you didn't think to look for a rain-out clause in the contract ... but a lawyer would have.

Until you're experienced with each type of contract you will be offered, you'd be smart to run them by an attorney who specializes in the music industry before you sign. You would also be wise to have an attorney draw up contracts that you will be offering to others—bandmember agreements, performance agreements (e.g. from the band to private-event clients), work-for-hire agreements with session players, and especially bandmember separation agreements—rather than trying to create your own based on samples from the internet. Most of these will be reusable as templates, so you won't have to pay the lawyer to write a new one each time, but as you get going, this will be part of your start-up expenses.

Below are a few other areas that deserve your full attention and careful organization. I'm offering you questions to consider but I'm not giving you the answers because I'm not an attorney or an accountant. Do your research and get advice from those professionals to make sure you're handling these situations correctly. Then use all of the organizational strategies you've learned in this book to set up systems for the options you choose to activate.

Thoughts to Ponder on Business Structure & Finances

Paying your musicians:

How will you decide how much to pay them? Should you pay them as employees or contractors? Do you need to withhold taxes from their pay? What are the consequences for you if you make the wrong decisions here?

Determining recording splits:

Have you joined a performing rights organization and do you understand how it works? Have you agreed on whether and how composition credits will be split? What about sound recording credits? There's a Recordings Tracker sample spreadsheet in Chapter 14 to get you started with tracking this data.

Collecting sales tax:

Do you need to charge sales tax on merch? Does it matter whether you're selling it in person or online? What do you do with sales tax if you do collect it?

Receiving tips, patronage, and crowdfunding income:

Are tips taxable? Do you know about tipping apps like Tipcow, including how to sign up with them and how the money is transferred to you? How is crowdfunding income regarded for tax purposes? Are there any write-offs available in crowdfunding projects? Are you aware of patronage models such as Patreon and the fan subscription option in Bandcamp in which fans give you money as general support, not necessarily for a specific project? How is that income counted and taxed, and what fees are withheld by the platforms?

Legacy planning:

Do you have a plan for what will happen to your royalties and other passive income when you die? That might seem like a worry for another decade, but it would be far better to start organizing it now than to try to reconstruct the data and splits years down the road, or even worse, leave it for your heirs to figure out. This is another good reason to use something like the Recordings Tracker spreadsheet in Chapter 14.

CHAPTER 7:

RELATIONSHIPS

It's hard to maintain relationships when you're single-mindedly pursuing your goals. When you're really in the zone, breaking away for a family dinner or friend's party or another band's gig is the last thing you want to do. Part of carving out time for your craft is managing your relationships so that your loved ones will understand your absences, whether you're locked in a room writing or away on tour.

It won't always work. Not everyone will tolerate not being your constant top priority. You'll have some difficult choices along the way, and you'll probably lose some connections with people who just can't deal with your divided attention. It could also happen that you will realize you don't want to be disconnected as much as some music careers require. If you derive a lot of joy from daily connection as a life partner or parent, a touring band is probably not the right path for you.

All of this is important to understand, because it impacts how you budget your time and how you steer the course of your career. If you can become aware of these dynamics early on, you'll save yourself missteps, restarts, heartache, and regrets down the road.

Who Are Your People?

You can think about all the people in your life in three basic groups: Inner circle, acquaintances, and fans.

Inner circle:

The people closest to you might be the ones who understand you the best, or they might never get this whole music thing you're doing. That partially depends on whether they're musicians too—if so, then naturally they'll be better able to relate. Some couples, families, and friends choose to be in bands together for this exact reason. In contrast, some know they would be at each other's throats and need to have their own separate projects. And you likely have some inner-circle folks who are not involved in music. Maybe they're family, maybe not; this is about who you're connected to by heart, not necessarily by blood or law. The challenge for you (a challenge you share with everyone pouring their entire being into their dream) is to build the career you want without destroying the relationships you value most.

Depending on the dynamics of your group, your bandmates might become as close as family or they might remain more distant, like typical coworkers. Either way, you will be spending a lot of time with them, so they will take on some sort of significance in your life.

Acquaintances:

Outside of your core circle of close relationships, you have a larger group of acquaintances: casual friends, peer musicians, industry professionals, and other people you are more loosely connected with. These are also relationships, but of a different sort. They don't require (or deserve, honestly) as much attention as your closest people, but they do still need some.

Also among these people are your networking contacts: A category of relationships that will evolve and grow over time and which will be essential to your success. More on that later in this chapter.

Fans:

There is another layer beyond acquaintances that is unique to entertainers: Fans, many of whom feel like they have a relationship with you. This is a one-way connection: Your music, and by extension, you, are meaningful to them but they themselves have little if any personal significance to you. Most fans get this and they're not offended or hurt by it, but they will often refer to themselves as "just" a fan. The absolute ideal for you is to make them feel valued—as a fan, but not "just" a fan—without implying that you really are true friends.

This doesn't mean you won't find new friends among your fans. Of course you will—it's one of the best parts of a music career! But there are two pitfalls that you'll do well to avoid:

1) Don't mislead a fan into thinking that you do actually consider him or her a friend if you don't. If you want to entice fans to help (for example with promotion), don't do it by teasing them with the possibility that it will give them access to your inner circle as a friend, or even worse, as a romantic interest.

2) Don't allow the distinction between fandom and two-way relationships to dissolve in your mind and life. It's a healthy boundary and it will become increasingly important as your career progresses, so be discerning about which fans you invite into your personal world.

We'll get more into this later on in the chapter with a section on fanbase building.

Relationship Equity

When people with whom you have a relationship feel good about you—like, love, trust, respect, appreciate, value, all of those things we want people to feel about us—what you have with them is called "relationship equity." Relationship equity is what you draw on when you ask for a favor, or for patience, or for another chance. Some people build relationship equity naturally: They're the ones everyone wants to help because they've always been there for others. They tend to offer help more often than they ask for it. They're almost always described as givers, even if they are so accomplished that they obviously must be devoting a lot of time to their own goals as well.

Of all the habits that either build or erode relationship equity, a surprising number are related to organization.

Eroding Equity: Habits That Undermine Relationships

Overpromising and underdelivering:

When the best of intentions meets an ugly end, this is often the reason. You might truly want and fully intend to do something in the moment that you promise it, but if you commit without considering whether you're capable of it, you've set yourself up to fail. Simply wanting to do it won't magically give you the power to do it. To be capable of keeping the promise, you need both the skills and the time, and only you can determine whether you have them. Deflecting blame by saying "you should have known I couldn't do that" or "you should have known it would take too long" is a cop-out. It's up to you to figure out from the beginning (ideally before you commit) whether you have both the skills and the time. If you're not sure about either, don't promise to do it. Promise to try, if that's acceptable in the situation and if you will actually try; otherwise be upfront and say they should find someone else to do it.

Overextending your energy:

If you need alone time before each gig, build in ways to ensure it for yourself. Make your needs clear in advance with your bandmates and any family and friends who will expect special attention at the show. Get procedures set with your volunteer or paid helpers before the day of the show and let them know you're trusting them to be self-sufficient with setup. Create a sign for the merch table that tells fans you'll be there for a Meet & Greet session after the last set. Patiently and preemptively setting boundaries is far better than trying to tough it out and ending up snapping at someone or being exhausted or irritated before you even hit the stage.

Failing to express gratitude:

If you spend most days just trying to keep your head above water, you might be so focused on your workload that you forget to appreciate help when you receive it. Maybe you feel like what someone did is too little/too late, or it's the least they could do, or the result isn't exactly what you wanted. Maybe the other person is calm and methodical, and what they're doing is simply what they always do, which makes it easy to take them for granted. Overwhelm makes people so reactive that they can forget to look at the big picture and notice who deserves a heartfelt thank-you.

Being more of a taker than a giver:

Desperate people use desperate measures. They take advantage of people's kindness or love for them, often say "I'll make it up to you," or take more than their fair share with the rationale that they need it the most. This is understandable in true emergencies, but if you live your life in perpetual crisis mode, or if you owe favors (or worse, money) to a lot of people, chances are your relationship equity is rather low.

•

Notice that I attributed the above examples to poor time management, which makes good people come across as unreliable or sometimes even selfish and thoughtless. We all know disorganization isn't always the reason for these habits. Some people are just users. If any of the above habits apply to you, I'm giving you the benefit of the doubt, but not everyone will assume the best about you. That's all the more reason that organizing your time is so important.

Building Equity: Habits That Sustain Relationships

Say thank you every chance you get:

If you regularly hear, "Oh, you don't have to thank me for that," you're doing it right. It's far better to say thank you as an extra courtesy than to fail to say it when it's due. Even better is when you can name what you're grateful for: "Hey, thanks so much for those photos. I love how you always capture non-weird facial expressions lol!"

Some people aren't in the habit of expressing appreciation. It doesn't mean they don't think it or feel it … for whatever reason, they just don't say it. If this is you, see if you can change this habit. Give some thought to why you might skip expressing gratitude. Was it used against you in the past? Some kids grow up in sarcastic families where saying "thank you" could get you a reply like, "Oh sure, I'm always happy to serve you." Others have been in relationships where saying thank you often drew a "but": "You're welcome, but that's the last time" or "You're welcome, but you really should be doing this yourself," etc. If that's been your reality, no wonder you're leery. It might take you a bit to learn that most people don't respond to appreciation that way.

Some people think they're expressing appreciation only to learn that it's not coming out that way. One of my clients had a habit of reminding me to do things that I don't need to be reminded of. Once when we were discussing the next phase of a project, we settled on the details and then he added one of those reminders. Somewhat exasperated, I said, "You don't need to tell me to do that. I always do that," to which he replied with a big smile, "I know you do. That's my way of telling you I like that you do that." If the people around you aren't the type to speak up like I did, you might think they know that you appreciate them when, actually, they're not so sure.

Be reliable:

This includes little things like being on time for meetings, calling back if you say you will, responding to messages, and sending the link or article that you said you would send. In a way, these little things are harder to do consistently than the big, high-consequence stuff because it's easy to believe it doesn't really matter. But there are crucial moments when these tiny things can make a difference in whether you'll receive an opportunity. If an overworked reporter needs a quote for a piece that's due in 20 minutes, he'll reach out to the source who will text or call right back and deliver an articulate response on the spot. If an event planner's nightmare client demands the addition of a live band to a huge event two days away, that planner will call the band with a track record of responsiveness and reliability. Last-minute crises happen all the time, and in those desperate moments, it's not about who might be the best person to quote or who's the best band in town: It's about who's most likely to come through and be the solution to the problem. Frankly, you earn those opportunities with organization, not with talent.

Communicate promptly:

If someone is waiting for information or an answer from you, send it as soon as you have it. As I'm writing this section, a musician just texted to ask if I can make his show tomorrow night. I know I can't, but I hate to disappoint him. It would have been easy not to answer and apologize later for missing it, but why? Why deprive him of known information that might impact his other decisions? There will be times when you need to withhold info from the public, for example some tour dates that are contingent on securing others or the impending departure of a bandmember, but unless it's a situation like that, don't keep people hanging.

Speak when you're spoken to:

This is related to the previous point. If your style is not to respond to messages and texts because in your mind it's understood that you received it/read it/agreed with it/whatever, know that not everyone thinks this way. Sorry, it's not enough that you have read receipts turned on. And don't just chalk this up to a generational difference. It's true that it's a more common complaint among people 40 and up, but I've also seen millennial-age show producers freak out over nonresponsive bands. A simple "thanks!" or "roger that" or thumbs-up emoji will prevent countless episodes of stress and resentment.

Be respectful of absolutely everyone:

This includes employees, interns, and volunteers anywhere you go, even if they got your order wrong; other musicians competing for the bookings you want; drunk fans acting like fools and grabbing at your setlist (or worse); and random people you don't expect to ever see again and their kids and dog. If it's got a heartbeat, put some respect on it. A stellar example of people living this value is the Peterson Brothers Band from Bastrop, TX. The group is fronted by brothers Glenn Jr. and Alex Peterson, ages 20 and 17 as of this writing, and despite their youth, you will never meet two more polite, courteous, patient, and appreciative musicians.

Know how to give efficiently:

"Giving til it hurts" is not something to aspire to. It doesn't get you more relationship equity—it just makes you less able to take care of yourself and have anything left for others. Far better and more sustainable than doing or giving more than you can spare is learning how to contribute one step that will help the other person to move forward and continue on their own. It can be as subtle as the difference between offering to track down a connection for someone vs. inviting them to call you if they want to pursue it. When you refine this skill, it will protect you from situations where you end up working harder on a person's problem or project than they do (a common pitfall that causes people to give up on networking or mentoring others).

Manage expectations:

Explain your process to your closest people. If you're an introvert and you need time alone, make sure your significant other knows it's not about him or her. If you need even more uninterrupted time to concentrate when you're writing or recording, explain this before someone disrupts your flow and causes an argument. If you're a touring musician just starting a romantic relationship, get clear from the beginning that you are often out of town. If friends and lovers don't go on tour with your band, don't try to change that now. (And if they do, please email me and tell me how y'all make that work. Not kidding.) Help your people to understand and cope with your absences and silences. Let them know when you'll be more available to them—Between tours? After the album comes out?—and keep any promises you make.

Business Building

Setting up your business on paper is one thing, but bringing it to life by involving other people is a whole new level. Even if you're a solo artist, you will need other people's help and support. Like most other businesses, yours will be built on relationships.

Band building:

We touched on the financial and legal aspects of assembling a band in the previous chapter. By this point you should know or be close to deciding how you want your band to be structured (one owner, two owners, all owners, etc.) Now let's consider the interpersonal part of it: Bringing together people who will mesh both operationally and creatively.

This process has the same challenges as hiring in any other field. You have to look at both job skills and personality traits and hope you're assessing correctly on both fronts. You need to know what you're looking for so you can spot it quickly, and at the same time you need to be open to discovering something that you didn't even know you wanted. You have to define the non-negotiable components of the job (guitar players must be able to play guitar) and also know what it is that you really want but would consider doing without if the person is otherwise a good fit (e.g. "experience preferred").

List both the absolutes and the negotiables before you start interviewing people. Otherwise you might be swayed by a charismatic personality and end up impulsively changing the direction you planned so carefully. I met a bandleader recently who acknowledged that their genre had never really been a fit for him, but a member he hired early on had detoured it through sheer force of personality. It was a fun ride, but now, years down the road, he's trying to figure out how to get back to his authentic, original intention.

If you have friends who have been through this before and you trust their judgment, you might consider asking them to help you with interviews and tryouts. Explain your direction and priorities to them so they can be looking for the same traits as you. Similarly, if you have friends in the local scene, ask them to put the word out that you're looking for bandmembers.

Before you start meeting with prospective bandmembers, coach yourself not to hire the first person who comes along just because you hate this awkward process and want it to be over. You might end up hiring that first interviewee, but it should be after you've also considered several others. You need to be able to turn people down; this won't be the last time you're in the position of hiring manager. Take care to be courteous about it, though: Chances are you will encounter each of these players again. Think of them not as rejected applicants but as new networking contacts.

When you do find the right person and you make the hire, do your best to keep communication open and to appreciate the person's contributions while also holding whatever boundaries, requirements, and expectations you established from the start. Over time, you might decide to change the requirements, making them either tighter or looser, which is normal in any business. You can be flexy when you start with a clear direction. All of your earlier values-assessing and goals-writing will keep you on track through the changes.

Being someone's boss or business partner and also a co-creator of art with them is a challenging dual role. Staying organized will become that much more valuable as you add more people to the mix.

Team building:

Over time you will start to accumulate a little posse of people who help you. They're the family and friends who support you with encouraging words and perhaps funding, the friends and fans who contribute their time at shows (merch volunteers, photo/videographers, social media amplifiers), the peers and mentors who answer your questions and help you find your direction, and the networking contacts who support you with important introductions. You might not realize at first that you actually have a team and these people are it, but when you do recognize it for what it is, you can start to organize them and get more benefit from their contributions.

One thing you'll remember fondly about the early days of your career is the people who were excited to help you simply because they believed in you. They weren't motivated by the possibility of hitching themselves to a celebrity's gravy train—they just wanted to support you because they loved you or your music or both. But don't think that the satisfaction of seeing you succeed is going to be enough to sustain their motivation. Especially if you can't pay them in money, you'll need to find other ways to reward them. You can come up with plenty of inexpensive ideas if you think ahead.

Here are some ways to appreciate your team members:

- Save your guest list spots for them and for media, not just for band friends or acquaintances who ask for a freebie.
- When they attend your shows and especially if they're doing a job for you there, thank them from the stage. Saying "thanks to Lucy for recording the show" and pointing her out over there in the corner will make Lucy feel great. All the better if the audience applauds. But don't do it in the middle of a song and create extra editing for Lucy. ;)
- List them on your website. You can do just first names or first and last. Check with them if you think they might prefer anonymity.
- Thank them in the credits on your recordings. That's a CD jacket they will cherish.
- Recognize them on your social media. Get photos with them to post as a thank-you after they do something extra-awesome, or just to fill in on your sites when there's no news to report.
- Share video clips from rehearsal and dedicate them to team members: ("Working on a new tune—Josie, bet you're gonna love this one")
- Follow their social media and show support for the other things that are important to them, projects they're working on, etc.
- Bring them swag from the road. This can be simple things like stickers from clubs you played or radio stations you visited, or CDs you traded with other bands on the bill … little things that don't cost you money or much space in your bag. Give that stuff to your hometown helpers. It's like saving the airplane pretzels for your kids—you might think it's nothing but they might think it's cool.
- Give them souvenirs from recording sessions. The normal debris generated in the studio can make clever gifts for your helpers—things like the tape from the mixing board with your band's name on it (autograph it and wrap it around a bottle of wine), or a guitar pick necklace that you made while you were fidgety during downtime, or a signed and dated rough-draft chart or lyrics page.
- Autograph a poster from a show they worked on and give it to them as a memento.
- Remember that what you consider trash from your day's work is gold to non-musicians. Setlists, for example: Even if it has beer stains and shoe prints, if it's got the date, the band name, and your autographs with a quick "Thanks for your help tonight!," that's a thoughtful token of your appreciation.
- Another trash-to-treasure item is worn-out drumheads. They make great wall art. The next time your drummer changes them out, slap a band sticker on each one, autograph them, and give them as gifts to your helpers. (These also make cool incentives in crowdfunding campaigns.)
- If a volunteer is with you for a long day, give them ten or twenty bucks to help cover a meal and gas. Bonus savings: If you know in advance that you'll have a helper with you and the gig includes drink tickets or meals for bandmembers and crew, include your helper in the food/drink headcount.
- Thank them collectively. When you do media interviews, drop in remarks about how so many of your fans help you with sharing your events and you have such a great team supporting the whole operation. This gives your volunteers public thanks and also encourages more people to share and support you.
- Have a volunteer event once a year. If you can cook or grill, do that. If not, get sandwich trays. Invest a hundred bucks for a low-key party and invite everyone who has given extra support. (Yes, this means you have to keep track of those names throughout the year.) Live-stream it or at least get some video clips and thank the team members who

live out of town or couldn't make the party.

- Alternatively (or do both!), designate one show a year for a private Volunteer Appreciation Afterparty. Make it a gig at a venue that has a green room and ask management in advance to let you stay an extra hour, spring for pizza and soft drinks, and invite your team to hang out backstage with the band.
- Aside from all of the above, look them in the eye and say thank you. Over time, the people who are helping you regularly will become fixtures with the band and you'll naturally start to take their presence for granted. That's ok—it's human. Remember to remind them once in a while that you still value them.

As time goes on, pay attention to who is bringing solid skills and reliability to their volunteer work for you. Really take note of the people who are doing jobs that require sustained focus and time commitment, like keeping up your website or overseeing your social media. These should be the first people you think about paying when you start to make enough money to hire out some of the work. Even if you can't pay them what the job is really worth, if they've been doing it for free, any amount will be like getting a raise.

Fanbase building:

Every business needs to build a customer base. If you want to learn more about it in general business terms, look up "customer acquisition" or "customer development." That's what fanbase building is for you. Chapter 11 on Promotion will give you a lot of direction on how to catch and hold fans' attention, but there are also things you can do apart from show-related activities that will help you build your fanbase, or tribe, or army, or whichever term best fits your vision.

One distinction you might find clarifying is that of the superfan. The term is sometimes used in a derogatory way to refer to obsessive fans, but it's more productive to think of it as the subset of your fans who are most enthusiastic about your work and most likely to help your efforts in some way. Superfans are more likely to tell their friends about you and encourage others to come to your shows or listen to your music. If they have any extra funds, they'll want to buy everything you sell—every album and single, every version of your band t-shirt. Even if there's something in your merch that they can't use or already have, they'll be inclined to buy it or buy another one and give it to someone else, and when they complete their collection of your merch, they'll keep throwing cash in the tip jar. They're also more likely to support your crowdfunding efforts and to help you as volunteers. So obviously, these are the fans you most want to identify and hold onto.

Some fans turn into superfans all on their own, simply because they're that blown away by your music and perhaps because it's in their nature to support and promote that which they appreciate. More often, though, fans become superfans because of something you've done that made them feel special. Maybe you gave them a birthday shoutout at a show or played a song they asked for with the "by special request" lead-in banter. Or maybe you remembered which of your songs is their favorite and made their night by spontaneously dedicating it to them (lova ya Jimi Lee and Ray Prim). Maybe you liked their comment on your post and made a witty reply. Maybe they were two bucks short and you let them have the CD anyway. This is the bottom-line reason for visiting with fans after shows, signing autographs and letting them take selfies with you even though you're sweaty and tired, and interacting on your social media instead of just using it as a billboard: All of that is meant to retain your fans and convert them to superfans when possible.

Another concept to keep an eye on is patronage: Essentially, it's people giving money to artists so you can spend time on your art vs. an unrelated day job. Patronage is not a new idea;

in fact, it was the way artists survived from ancient times until well into the 1800s, and beyond that it has continued to some extent with grantmaking in fields like literature but not so much in non-classical music. The good news for indie musicians is that the practice is now making a comeback in a modified form which once again supports music: In the past, individual artists would have one or more wealthy patrons who gave them money to live on and create their art. Now, rather than having one or a few ultra-wealthy patrons, artists are connecting with groups that provide a form of collective patronage. For example, Black Fret, which began in Austin and is in development to expand into other U.S. cities, pools money from members to give grants to musicians in their local community. Web-based groups like Patreon are focused primarily on establishing patronage for musicians, and some indie music discovery sites including Bandcamp have added the option to subscribe to individual musicians, which provides them with steady income as they continue to create new music.

We'll continue with fanbase strategies in Chapter 11: Promotion.

Networking

If I had a dollar for every time I've been told that musicians hate networking…. Let's get past that, can we? Networking is not sales. It's not aggressive. It's not about storming a room or emailing relentlessly and hounding people to do stuff for you. That's a sure way to burn bridges, not build them. Networking is making the most of your relationships to ensure that everyone knows about your musical goals and identifying those who are willing to support you in some way and will actually act on that willingness when the time comes.

It can be casual or formal, individual or group-structured. You're already doing it if you go to music meetups or attend music-biz conferences. Catching other bands' shows or having coffee or lunch with other artists, industry acquaintances, and even contacts outside of music might be things you already do and didn't realize they count as networking.

Networking can seem mysterious and intimidating until you realize that it's basically just being nice to people and giving them opportunities to be nice to you in return. Some would argue that it's also about developing strategic alliances that will elevate you above others, positioning you as the winner and others as losers by default. Taken to the furthest extreme, that view of networking is more accurately called game-playing or political maneuvering. Either way, whether you see the interpersonal strategies of the music business as collaborative or competitive, it really is often about "who you know."

Networking is an important element of "relational promotion," which we'll cover in depth in Chapter 11.

Conscious connecting:

Networking is an intentional activity. More than casual hanging out or just being out in the scene, networking is done with a plan, a strategy, and the conscious purpose of making and maintaining connections that will help your career. It can be very formally structured, like groups that have attendance requirements and quotas for referrals, or totally casual, like hanging out with friends but remembering to tell them about your upcoming show. It's something that starts to come naturally for self-employed people, especially once you realize that it's about collaborating, not relentlessly pestering people to help you.

Networking is a long game. It takes time for people to get to know you, even if only as an acquaintance, and to start developing trust and goodwill born out of that familiarity. In fact, one of the basic tenets of business networking is referred to as the "know, like, and trust" factor, originally expressed by master networker Bob Burg: "All things being equal, people do business with, and refer business to, those people they know, like and trust."

So it's true that getting ahead is mostly about who you know. That sentiment is usually expressed as a negative, conjuring images of people giving the best opportunities to their relatives and side pieces, but it's often (perhaps more often) true that "who you know" comes from consistently being around to help others and receive opportunities. Proximity equals opportunity, I like to say.

A slightly different perspective on "who you know" is "who knows you." The more you get out, both to perform and to interact with your music community, the more likely you are to come to the attention of the tastemakers: The people who have the ear of reporters, bookers, music patrons, and other influential figures. This is how buzz begins to build for your act.

Another classic networking concept and strategy is "givers gain," from Ivan Misner. The idea is that you start out every networking encounter with the intention of finding a way to help each person you speak to. That help can be as simple as suggesting an article to read or a Twitter account to follow, or offering to make an introduction to someone the person would benefit from meeting. What you're giving costs you nothing more than a few minutes of your time, and it could generate money or opportunity for the recipient. Make a habit of that and people will eventually want to do it for you too. Some will think of ways to help you and offer those ideas out of the blue; with others, you'll be able to ask for their help and they will happily give it.

Here's an example of networking that worked out very well:

A few years ago, I joined the National Academy of Recording Arts and Sciences, or NARAS, best known as the organization behind the Grammy Awards. That summer, I attended a NARAS networking luncheon during the Viva Big Bend Festival in West Texas. A client band of mine, Soul Track Mind, was on the festival bill the next night, but I traveled ahead a day early to network at the NARAS meetup. There I met a nice couple, veteran live audio producer Malcolm Harper and his wife, Deborah, and invited them to see STM's headlining set. The band delivered a face-melting performance and made a great impression on the Harpers.

Soon after that, the Harpers invited me to their home to visit and tour Malcolm's studio (built in a semi-trailer to take onsite for huge productions like the ACL Music Festival and NCAA Final Four broadcasts). As we chatted over sweet tea, Malcolm recalled a competition over in Louisiana that a friend of his was involved with called the Music Prize, and suggested that I enter STM. He said the Music Prize folks wanted to get the word out that entry was not limited to Louisiana residents, so it would help them if a Texas-based band signed up.

I checked it out and we entered. STM won the competition, which included a cash prize and two days of full-service recording at Brady Blade's revered studio in Shreveport. One of the judges, Grammy winner Lawrence "Boo" Mitchell, was so impressed that he added to the prize package with two days of free recording, engineering, and production at his historic Royal Studios in Memphis. With the Blade and Royal sessions as anchors, we put together a regional tour the following spring with stops at the two studios plus seven performances including two festivals along the way, culminating with a South By Southwest showcase. More than an album's worth of recordings came out of that period, and all of the relationships in this chain of events are ongoing and productive to this day.

Stated another way, networking lined up a huge opportunity for the band, they sealed the deal with stellar musicianship and showmanship, and the connections have produced still more opportunities on all sides. That's a picture-perfect networking outcome.

Getting started with networking:

- Find an upcoming event or meetup that is intended specifically for networking. That way, everyone will be there for the same purpose and you won't feel (as) weird about walking up to strangers and introducing yourself. You might even get away with waiting for them to approach you.

- Go in with the attitude that you're there to see who you can help. Of course you're also there to find people who can help you, but that comes later.

- Understand that a "win" at this does not mean someone you met there hired you. Networking is not selling to the room. That's a pitch session—very different. Networking is informing everyone about what you do so they can refer you to other people they know. It's the difference between, "Please hire me to play your party" (wrong) and "Please keep me in mind when someone you know needs a band for their party" (right). Going in with this perspective will naturally prevent you from being pushy or salesy.

- Speaking of that, avoid people who are pushy or salesy. They're not doing it right. Networking does not require you to hire or buy directly from the people you network with, unless you really, honestly want and need what they have.

- Show genuine interest in people. I don't mean act genuine and get really good at pretending you're interested in people. That will just make you hate networking so much that you'll never do it. If you dread getting trapped in conversations that don't interest you, practice getting out of them. One of the best ways is to bring someone else into the conversation and then excuse yourself. (My clients and colleagues know they can tag me in like this when they get cornered.)

- If you're very uncomfortable with this whole thing and hate the idea of being stuck there for an hour or more, give yourself permission to leave as soon as you've had a basic conversation with three people. Or two, or one. Start where you can. Next time, make it one additional person. Eventually you won't need the escape quota.

- Be ready for the "elevator speeches." They're called that because they're meant to be brief enough that you could say the entire thing in the time it takes to ride a few floors together in an elevator. They usually happen at sit-down events such as lunches and group meetings, and usually not at happy hours and stand-up/walk-around mixers. This is a core networking activity, so you're going to have to do it sooner or later. In the beginning, it's fine if you stick with this simple script: "Hi, I'm Joe Smith and I'm a professional [drummer/guitarist/vocalist/musician]. I'm new to networking, so I'm just here to meet new people and start making connections. Thanks." Depending on the group, some kind soul might ask you a useful follow-up question like, "Are you in a band?" "What type of music do you play?" etc.

- Listen to everyone else's elevator speeches and pay attention to what line of work they're in. The more experienced networkers will often ask for a specific introduction or resource, or say, "A good referral for me is...." With each one, try to think of a way you could connect them with someone who has what they need. (This is just a mental exercise. You're not expected to actually fulfill everyone's needs.)

- Choose one person to talk to after the structured part of the meeting is done. It can be someone with a similar career, an interesting-sounding job, or just a friendly attitude. Major bonus points if you choose someone you can help with information or a referral. Then talk to that person. If you hit it off, ask for a business card so you can follow up with her or him.

- Follow up later that day or the next day. This is not dating. Don't play games like waiting so you don't seem too interested. That's not necessary or respected in networking.

- Do NOT take the email addresses from the business cards you collected and add them to your newsletter or promotional mailing list. That's a major networking gaffe. You probably will get added to other people's mailing lists without your permission, and you can feel free to unsubscribe or even block the person if necessary.

Should you join a networking group?

There are groups that exist for the distinct purpose of networking, and then there are all the other groups in existence that aren't necessarily for networking but can be used that way. You've got options:

- Structured referral-sharing groups: The best-known of these is BNI, which has chapters everywhere. Groups like this have dues, regular meetings (usually weekly and often at the crack of dawn) that you are required to attend, and quotas of referrals you have to make to other members. This type of group is usually not useful for DIY musicians, unless you join as part of a day job in a field like real estate, insurance, finance, or sales.

- No-quota groups: Some networking groups take elements of the more formal groups but eliminate the dues, attendance requirements, and referral quotas. These are often advertised on Meetup or LinkedIn, and might have a small fee per meeting. This type of group can be a great resource. Look for ones that have a theme that connects in some way to what you need and try out a meeting. If it seems to be well-run, well-attended, and at a realistic time of day, consider making the group a priority to attend regularly. You don't have to go every time they meet—just often enough to be remembered by the members.

- Virtual groups: These can be a useful supplement to in-person groups. They're not the greatest for initiating contact and it can be harder to convert them into real-life connections, but they're very handy for reinforcing connections with people you've already met in person. If you're new to networking and still feeling awkward about it, groups like this enable you to read others' conversations without participating, so you can sometimes learn about opportunities without having to talk to a lot of people.

- One-off events: Workshops, speeches, and special-occasion happy hours are all excellent for networking. Here in Austin, Texas, we have dozens of these every day, so the challenge is choosing among them and not spending too much time trying to make them all. If you don't live in a "music city," you'll have to dig a bit deeper to find these events. Look for nonprofit associations that support the arts, departments of local government that put on small classes or mixers, and private businesses that host informational gatherings. If you have a college or university nearby, look for events put on by their various departments or as part of their community outreach efforts. Remember, the event theme doesn't have to be music-related—think creatively about how various business themes might attract people who have the information or connections you need.

- Professional associations: If you have a chapter of the National Academy of Recording Arts and Sciences (NARAS, a.k.a. the Grammys) near you, consider joining. Membership grants you access to events attended by artists, producers, and industry folks who are farther along in their careers. Find out who the elected leaders are in the chapter and make a point of meeting them: They are often inclined toward mentoring newer artists.

- Peer groups: This is your best bet for developing alliances with other musicians in your town. Songwriters' groups, artists' collectives, and song-swap performances all fit this category. Like any small, loosely run group, these can be great or they can be petty and counterproductive. Find the ones that work for you and get out of bad ones as gracefully as possible without burning bridges. If you feel moved to volunteer or even start a group, remember to think of time as a resource just like money and only spend what you can afford.

Advanced networking skills:

- Whenever you meet someone whose contact info you want to keep, jot down what stood out to you about the person. Write it on their business card, put it in your digital contacts, add a note to your calendar entry for the event where you met them, etc. It doesn't have to be the most relevant info, just the thing that made an impression. It might be that they have red hair or they're into skydiving or have a pet chinchilla. Don't think of this as a test or an obligation—it's just a way of remembering who was who.

- You don't have to keep every card you're given. If you can't think of a way to help them, can't think of a way they can help you, and didn't click with them as a person, it's OK to toss it.

- Regarding people you network with regularly, know what's important to them right now: It could be a project they're immersed in, something they're looking for, or something going on personally (new baby, parent's illness). Social media is useful for keeping casual tabs on more people than you thought possible. Try to remember what matters to them and ask about it, but don't be fake. This is meant to be a way of showing genuine interest, not creeping.

- Introduce by "name and fame": When you introduce someone you know to a third person, give their full name and what they do, framed in a bit of why they're impressive. Examples: "This is Malcolm Harper, owner of Reelsound Recording which live-streamed ACL Fest last year"; "This is Boo Mitchell, owner of Royal Studios in Memphis where Al Green made all of his iconic recordings." The best is when you can introduce two people to each other this way. They'll both be flattered and appreciative that you did the bragging for them. That's master-level networking.

- Add an "ask" to your elevator speech: "Hi, I'm Victor Celania and I'm the leader of a swing band called The Waller Creek Vipers. A great referral for me is the person who plans their company holiday party." Make it one very specific example, not general like "anyone who hires bands." In fact, if you use the word "anyone," you're probably doing it wrong. This specificity works because it gets people thinking about real people they know, not everyone who might theoretically hire you. Have different "asks" ready to go for various groups and purposes.

- Outside of networking events, make warm introductions between people by email, LinkedIn, Facebook message, or whatever method is most appropriate. Use "name and fame" and include something about why you recommend them or believe they should know each other.

- Support your networking contacts (both individuals and groups) on social media: Like their pages, follow them on Twitter or Instagram, connect with them on LinkedIn if you use it. You don't have to put them on notification and respond to everything they share, but keep them in your newsfeed and react to their posts when the spirit moves you.

- And finally, the mother of all networking activities—the "one-on-one": You might have thought it was just having lunch or coffee. Nope, there's a world of technique and etiquette to this. Here are the highlights:
  - When you invite someone to lunch or coffee, say it in a way that makes clear you want it to be a networking meeting. Something like, "I'd like to learn more about your work and tell you a bit more about mine. Could we get together for coffee?" This emphasizes that you have a specific agenda and it's not a date.
  - Do not ask if you can "pick their brain." Even if you intend to buy the meal. Unless

you have an established relationship with this person, you will be perceived as asking for a free dose of the expertise that other people pay them for. That's insulting. If you really do want advice and you have no intel to offer in return (in other words, this person is far beyond you in experience), say it like this: "I would be grateful for some of your time. What is your consultation rate?" If they come back with a number, arrange an amount of time that you can afford. If they respond with something like, "Thanks for offering to pay, I appreciate the courtesy, but I don't mind giving you 15 minutes on the phone," take it guilt-free and know that you've made a good impression.

- o   If you requested the meeting and they ask you to suggest the place, go for a coffee or sandwich shop near them. If the other person reached out to you and asks where you want to meet, suggest the same type of place about halfway between your home base and theirs, or go closer to them if you don't mind.
- o   Be on time. If you are actually getting a coffee or a meal, get there early so you don't burn meeting time with ordering. It's standard that each person pays their own bill, but feel free to buy for them if you've invited them out to thank them for a favor or referral. Don't do it as a bribe—that's weasely.
- o   When the person arrives, ask how much time they have. Then plan on 1/3 of the time to ask about their business, 1/3 to talk about your business, and 1/3 to just visit (not necessarily in that order). This is not a secret calculation that everyone else knows; most people aren't this organized about networking. But you, master networker, will create maximum efficiency and maximum goodwill if you guide the conversation in this way.
- o   Ask them who they need to meet. It could be specific individuals or people in particular roles. Occasionally you'll know someone that you can connect them with on the spot, but usually this is info that you'll keep in mind for future as you grow your network. Then tell them the same for yourself.
- o   If the meeting went well, ask the best way to keep in touch. Do they use social media? Are there groups they go to regularly? Then reach out to them if you have something to offer or just to say hello now and then, but don't overdo it. Most people will remain cordial acquaintances, which is fine. If it turns out that you have a lot to share with each other, you will naturally build a closer alliance over time.

There's a lot more that can be said about networking. If this piqued your interest and you want to learn more, you might start with Dale Carnegie's classic book, *How to Win Friends and Influence People.* It's old, the language is pretty corny by today's standards, and you'll have to keep reminding yourself how traditional business lessons apply to your DIY music career, but the advice is solid.

Thoughts to Ponder on Relationships

Network before you're "ready":

You don't have to wait until you've got your entire career mapped out to start networking. You can begin building relationships even if you don't have anything specific to ask for yet. In fact, it's better to start now because the point of networking, as you now know, is to build relationship equity. So meet people and start thinking of ways they'll eventually be resources for you, but for now, look for ways to be a resource to them. When the time comes to ask them for help, you'll already have equity banked with them.

Revolving team members:

Team members will come and go. Bandmembers might too. This is another reason that it's worth your while to document all of your procedures. You don't want any part of your operation fully dependent on the memory skills or involvement of one person, even if it's a bandmember.

Namechecks:

Get in the habit of publicly thanking people by name. It will serve you well even when you're successful enough to pay your help. Down the road, your Grammy acceptance speech will write itself.

Warm is better than cold:

When you know someone that a new connection would like to meet and you introduce them, it's called a "warm" introduction because they both already know (and ideally like and trust) you. Without you as the link, the person hoping to make the connection would have to do a "cold" outreach to the target person and wouldn't get the benefit of being presented by a known entity.

Keeping track of contacts:

Networking doesn't work very well if you don't have some way of organizing your contacts and remembering to stay in touch. This puts networking in the realms of both data organization and time management. Look for a sample Networking Contacts spreadsheet in Chapter 14.

The annoyingly productive helper:

Say you have a real go-getter of a helper who is blazing through tasks, clearing obstacles, accessing new opportunities, and coming back to you saying s/he needs the deliverables you promised—the copy you were supposed to write, the songs you were supposed to finish, the video shoot you've been putting off, etc. If you resent that person for "pushing" you, maybe you need to talk about a more manageable pace. But here's another possibility to consider: Perhaps you're irritated because s/he's eliminating your excuses, fulfilling every "If I only had [a Facebook page/booking connections/a promo video]," and now you have to actually do what you've always said you would do if not for those obstacles. Time to put up or shut up.

CHAPTER 8:

COMMUNICATION

Communication is like an audio mix: When it's good, you don't notice it because it's doing its job of letting every sound be heard; when it's bad, it's highly noticeable and everyone has a different opinion on how to fix it.

Flawed communication can suffocate any band or solo career. You need to be able to express yourself both intellectually (conveying facts, logistics, and strategies) and emotionally (disagreeing without fighting, being honest about fears, hopes, hurts, and passions) as well as artistically, and you need to work with people who can do the same.

What's Your Communication Style?

Do you prefer to talk to people in person, by phone, or by message (email, text, social media messenger)? How available are you for each method? Do you usually respond quickly or take your time, even if it's not something you need to think over? Are you more of an extrovert who is energized by interacting with people or an introvert who needs plenty of time alone to recharge?

If you're a one-person operation, you'll have to handle the communication yourself, whether you're well-suited for it or not. Understanding your strengths, limitations, and preferences in this realm will help you to communicate in the ways that are most effective for you. If you're not a solo act, you have the option to let band communication be someone else's job. You'll still have to do as well as you can with reaching out and responding on your own behalf, but you can at least offload the responsibility of doing it on behalf of the entire project.

Choose a Communicator

Save yourself a never-ending headache and designate one person to be the band's communicator. This role is threefold: convey information from the band to the outside world; convey information from the outside world to the band; and convey information from the band's decision-makers to all bandmembers. This is the person who is responsible for making sure everyone receives the info they're supposed to receive.

I'm sure I don't need to tell you how important this job is.

The communicator will probably be the bandleader, at least in the beginning. As the band develops, another member might turn out to be a fit for this job. (Not to reinforce stereotypes, but drummers are often good at this.) As you grow, you might be able to hire someone to do this job for the band. If you acquire a manager, communication might become part of that person's job, depending on how you define the parameters of the management relationship.

If you're doing your own booking and PR, the communicator is the point of contact for those tasks. S/he's the one reaching out to, and responding to, talent buyers, promoters, producers, sound engineers, and the media. This is the cradle-to-grave contact for every gig, from initial booking inquiry, to confirming and adding the show to the band calendar and all online calendar listing sites, to advancing promo materials and stage plot & inputs to the venue, to promoting the show on social media, to fielding calls and texts the day of the show, to making sure everyone gets their meal and drink tickets, to getting everyone to the stage, to making sure settlement is completed at the end. If you're outsourcing booking or PR, the communicator is the liaison for your outside booker and publicist and will still be the one handling all of the ground-level interactions around each gig.

Within the band, this is the person conveying all operational information and making sure everyone has received it, both with day-to-day functioning and show advancing. If anyone has a question about an upcoming gig, a reserved date in the calendar, a media appearance, whether rehearsal is on, whether that one stupidly early soundcheck got changed, or whether the show tonight is backlined, the communicator is the person to ask for the official answer.

Why must there be only one?

It's most efficient to have one person handling all communication for several reasons:

- It prevents duplication of effort ("hey guys, somebody sent something about the Dallas show next week but I can't find it, can somebody resend?")
- It prevents confusion among outsiders ("for booking, call Greg; for show promotion, call Joe; for media inquiries, call Briane")
- It prevents errors introduced when information is passed through a string of people, a.k.a. the Telephone Game

Why couldn't you divide the work more evenly and have, say, one bandmember be the contact for booking and another be the contact for promotion? In my experience, here's what that will look like:

The band's booking member (A) works with the venue's talent buyer (B) to confirm the gig. A then gets an email from the venue's marketing director (C) looking for an advance of promo materials. A replies to C, copying the bandmember in charge of promotion (D), and tells C that D handles promo. D sends C the files she requested. So far so good: A with B and C with D. But then, one week later, C emails A (not D) to ask for an additional item. A again forwards C's email to D. Meanwhile, B emails D (not A, because C erroneously told B that D is the new contact for the band) with a proposed update on the set time, but her email goes unnoticed because D has never corresponded with B and didn't have her email address set to be marked as important. Another week goes by and B, now annoyed, sends another email to D (not A) about the set time. D sees B's email this time and replies to her, copying A, and tells her that A handles the booking details. B replies to both A and D, hoping someone will just answer the question and already thinking this band had better draw well because they're a pain in the ass to book. The next day, A (not D) gets an email from C about the show's Facebook event.

See?

All communication goes through one person to reduce confusion and missed connections among people contacting the band, people the band is contacting, and bandmembers themselves trying to keep up with what's going on. Now, you could say that the venue reps (B and C) in the above example were the poor communicators and the bandmembers (A and D) were clear throughout, and you'd be right. But do you want to be right or do you want to be booked?

But seriously, one all-powerful communicator?...

Having a single communicator doesn't mean that person has to be empowered to make all of the band's decisions or to function in isolation. You can require that all bookings be confirmed within the band before the communicator commits to them with the talent buyer (although that will greatly impede the communicator's efficiency; better to give them reserved dates to fill within preset parameters). You can also have the communicator copy every bandmember on every email if you want (although you will probably regret that rather quickly). If the communicator is not the bandleader or owner, it would make sense for him or her to at least forward finalized email strings to the leader/owner as FYIs.

Whoever you choose to be the communicator, stick with the choice. Everyone needs to respect the path of communication and not jump in and start telling members what to do if they're not the communicator. This includes the bandleader and/or band owner(s)—if you're the boss and you appointed someone else to be the communicator, even you need to speak through that person to convey operational info.

As a safety net, make sure someone else has the login credentials for the communicator's band email account. If the communicator gets hit by a bus or runs away to the Peace Corps, you'll need to be able to pick up where s/he left off with all of the band correspondence.

Plan for Others' Lack of Communication

Getting organized is like quitting smoking and then finding the smell of other people's smoke to be much more obvious. The more proactive and dependable you become with communication, the more you will notice that most of the world isn't that great at it. Your nimble action and reactions will give you an advantage, but exchanges will rarely happen as quickly and efficiently as you're now capable of because you'll be waiting for replies from others.

When you get reliable systems in place, you'll become consistently more organized than everybody else. You'll have to put safeties in place for the times when others mess up and need to catch up, because often those others will be the people with the power to get you what you want. Being the most organized person in the equation is not an entirely comfortable feeling, but it's better than the alternative.

Often the last round of messages in a conversation gets neglected. Final questions and "oh by the way"s get left hanging. When the convo is logistical (e.g. with a promoter about an upcoming show), plan what you will do if you never get an answer to those last questions. If you've asked a couple times and you don't have time to wait any longer, tell them what you'll do if you don't hear back. Don't be snippy or rude about it, of course. Example:

"Hey John, another quick follow-up. Hoping you can get back to me with our load-in/check times for our 9pm set tomorrow. If we don't hear from ya, we'll be there at 7pm."

Sometimes this will trigger a response, either because they need something different and now realize it hasn't been expressed, or because what you've proposed is fine and you've made it easy for them to rubber-stamp it. If you still don't get a response, do exactly what you said you would do and roll with the situation when you get there. Worst-case scenario, you have a message trail to show that you tried.

You can use the same approach with bandmembers, but if you're the leader you have the authority to require better responsiveness from them, and also the obligation: Poor communication will sink a band, even if the musical product is brilliant.

"S/he's probably just busy":

Make this your default assumption every time someone fails to answer you. Say it to yourself if you start to feel insecure or rejected over unanswered booking or media pitches, requests for help or input, even inquiries to vendors you're trying to hire. Say it when you're irritated at bandmembers, talent buyers, sound engineers, and promoters who are slow to answer or who fall silent in the middle of a project you're already working on. Say it when you're feeling awkward after you've reached out to someone you'd like to network with or be mentored by and you haven't heard back.

I really want you to understand this. Not just hope it's true or take it as encouragement, but fully integrate this as fact. So I'm going to pull out the heavy artillery and paraphrase Liam Neeson: I possess a very particular set of skills. Skills I have acquired over a very long career. Skills that qualify me to tell you: They are almost always just busy.

When you understand this, outreach becomes cooperative instead of competitive. You stop feeling rejected or inconvenienced and start empathizing with their struggle. Paradoxically, people become more likely to respond because this perspective makes you much more approachable. It colors the tone of your emails, texts, and voicemails; changes your word choices from demanding and entitled to patient and appreciative; impacts your timing and frequency; and lets them know that when they do finally respond, even if the answer isn't what you wanted, you won't be a jerk about it. Most important, this attitude of empathy for the people you're approaching shores up your motivation to keep trying to connect, whether with these contacts or with new ones.

The Monster That Is Email

I don't know anyone who loves email. I think it's safe to say that the vast majority of email users see it as valuable but extremely high-maintenance, and a significant number consider it a full-on nightmare. No matter how you feel about it, email is essential to your business, so you have no choice but to learn how to manage it. It can be conquered, but you must know your opponent. Here are a few points to help you knock it down to size.

The one thing that matters:

Your email system has one crucial job: To prevent you from missing important emails. That's it. All the other stuff is window dressing. As you develop and continuously refine your process for dealing with email, you'll stay sane if you remember that this is the only thing it absolutely must accomplish. Beyond that, you have a lot of options for clearing your inbox and organizing what remains.

Extracting important emails:

You can create a reliable method for separating out the important emails without having to clear your entire backlog and start with an empty inbox. Follow these steps now and chip away at decluttering later.
- Define "important." Remember earlier when we talked about urgent vs. important? Urgent means time-sensitive and important means it has consequences. Everything in an email inbox feels urgent simply because it has an arrival date and time (and the screamy subject lines don't help). Importance is defined in so many different ways that

it's hard to apply equitably from one email to the next. Seen side by side in your inbox, the "SALE ENDS TONIGHT!" email from your favorite gearhead site and the "SUBMISSIONS CLOSE TONIGHT!" email from that festival you want to get on both trigger the urgent + important response in your mind. Get very clear on what types of email you consider important.

- Choose one and only one way to mark important emails and stick with it. Using stars AND flags AND the unread status doesn't make emails stand out—too much variety makes them blend in. Choose one of those things—flag or star (in a single color) or unread status—and keep it meaningful by using it ONLY on important emails.

- Schedule time to work on email. Even if you're looking at it throughout the day, set aside some dedicated time, daily or close to daily, to double-check that nothing important has slipped by. Once you get up to speed with this and if you maintain it consistently, it should only take a few minutes.

- Keep up with blocking and deleting unwanted mail. Unsubscribing doesn't always work (big surprise), and blocking specific addresses or filtering them to the trash also doesn't always work because groups sometimes send from a different address each time. Make use of the filtering and blocking options in your email app, but don't spend so much time on them that they become more of a project than they're worth. You'll still have individual emails to delete day after day.

- Use tags, filters, and folders to set aside emails you're done working on but want to save. Make folders by category if you think it's worth it, but even just one called "Emails to Save" is better than leaving them loose in your inbox.

- Set realistic expectations going forward. Decide how cluttery you'll let your email be. This is a stellar example of the value of being "organized enough." Getting to an empty inbox every day might be realistic for you with a reasonable amount of self-discipline, or it might not be worth the effort. A lot depends on how much email you receive. If you use it only for your music career, you'll get less than if you also use it heavily in your day job. The volume coming at you also depends on how good your spam filter is and how many marketing lists your address is on.

Delegation

I've included delegation in the Communication chapter because communication is the key to making it work. Delegation is assigning a job to someone else. It's not the same as relinquishing responsibility for the job. If the job was never yours in the first place, passing it on to someone else isn't delegation.

Delegating a job is like subletting your apartment: Even if you're not living there, you're still the one responsible for making the rent payment. When you delegate a job to someone else, you remain responsible for ensuring it is completed. This means you need to communicate the deadline and instructions for completing it and make sure it's done correctly and on time.

There are some types of sub-projects that can be delegated to another bandmember, with communication handled by the other person. This can work fine with things done completely behind the scenes like recording, where one member takes the lead on all of the back and forth emails with the studio, engineer/producer, mastering engineer, cover art designer, and pressing plant. Keep in mind that if you're playing shows in the same timeframe that you're recording, you'll have an extra coordination challenge in the band calendar, but aside from that, the communication around a separate sub-project like this can be handled by another member to take some of the load off of the designated band communicator.

Another sub-project that can be handled by someone other than the communicator is booking transportation and lodging for a tour. These arrangements are contingent on the gig bookings and rarely involve communication with a talent buyer or venue, so there should be no crossed wires between the band communicator and the helper who is booking hotels and the van or flights based on what the communicator is adding to the band calendar.

As you continue to gel as a band, you'll learn which members are willing and able to take on some admin duties and possibly start to find more opportunities for delegation. This is great when it happens because it redistributes the load. If it doesn't happen, though, don't force it. If you're the band owner and no one else is as motivated as you to persist with the booking push or the PR push, you're better off keeping an inordinate amount of the work on your own plate and finding volunteers outside of the band vs. pressuring a bandmember to do something s/he really doesn't want to do. If members' pay has been structured to compensate them for sharing the admin load and they're not sharing, that's an imbalance that needs to be addressed. But if they are solely side players with no investment in the band, you can't really expect them to do more than learn, rehearse, and perform the music.

Beware of things that are "everybody's job." When something is supposed to be done equally by everyone, one of three things will happen:

1. Nobody will do it.
2. One person will do it all the time, resent the hell out of it, and periodically blow up at everyone else for not doing their fair share.
3. Everyone will do it equally because one person is supervising the operation and forcing everyone to take their turn. When that happens, it's not actually "everybody's job": It's the job of the supervisor, and the supervisor has delegated it to everybody else.

Never designate something as "everybody's job" and leave it at that. Skip all the drama and choose one person to either do the job themselves or to supervise the delegation.

Thoughts to Ponder on Communication

Key forms to keep handy:

In addition to your usual promo assets and stage plot & inputs, have a completed and signed W-9 available to email to bookers who need one from the band.

Too many emails is better than too few:

You might resent being included in email strings that have little to do with you, until the day when you need a crucial piece of info and discover you weren't copied on that email. You can make them more tolerable by putting filters in place to file emails that are informational only, so they're not in the way of your more active conversations.

By the same token, remember to copy others as needed whenever you send an email.

Good sound starts well before soundcheck:

Some sound engineers actually want to hear from you before soundcheck. "I hate to show up to a gig not having talked to the band, not having seen their input list or stage plot and not really knowing anything about them," says Hi Q Production owner Eric Harrison. "If I don't talk to the band, I'll go online and look them up and be like, alright this is probably what's going to happen. But that's huge when I can talk to somebody, they can hear my voice, and then, the day of, everybody's so much more relaxed because they already have confidence in you that's it's going to go well."

Do you need business cards?

Yes. Show postcards and flyers are not an adequate replacement for this. You need a card with your name, your band or company name, and your contact info (at least email). It doesn't have to be a traditional-looking white card with basic fonts: There are tons of cool designs. Go crazy with the colors and art, but make sure the print isn't too small to read. People will often want to write on the card you give them, so avoid solid dark backgrounds and get matte instead of glossy finish, at least on the back. Stick with standard sizes so they'll fit in people's wallets or business card binders (yes, some of us networking nerds have these)—the trendy smaller cards are too easy to lose.

You don't have to spend a lot of money on this. There are many inexpensive online business card printers, and many local print shops offer affordable options too.

CHAPTER 9:

BOOKING & TOURING

Did you skip straight to this chapter? I know, booking is a common pain point. But seriously, you'll get much more out of this chapter if you read all the previous ones too.

•

This is one of my very favorite parts of music business administration. I know, I'm a freak. Nobody loves booking and tour routing. But I do. It's an organizer's dream job.

I'm sorry that you're probably not going to love it, but I'll do my best to at least help you hate it less. With this chapter, you're going to make heavy use of your data organization, time management, and networking skills and tools.

Where to Begin?

OK. You opened a fresh browser tab and a blank email, and you're wondering where to start. The world (or maybe just your city for now) is your oyster. What do you do first?

Before you start looking up venues and sending booking inquiries, have you answered these questions?

When you picture yourself living the dream, what does your fantasy audience look like? An outdoor amphitheater full of teens to thirtysomethings? An auditorium packed with screaming fangirls? Or a steamy nightclub packed with over-21s dancing and drinking? A grand ballroom dance floor, or a mosh pit? How about tables of elegant couples sipping cocktails? Families enjoying a good meal or a day at the fair? Or a small group of people in a pin-drop-quiet room giving your music their full attention?

What kind of music do you want to play? Do you prefer to play your originals? Are you open to playing covers? Or do you in fact prefer covers? Do you sing, or is your music strictly instrumental? Do you want to play your preferred genre, even if it's not a fit for some places you might be able to get booked?

All of these questions indicate what types of venues and talent buyers you'll be pursuing to book you, whether it's for festivals and outdoor stages, nightclubs, dance clubs, restaurants, bars, private corporate events and weddings, or listening rooms and house concerts. As you would when applying for jobs in other fields, don't try for anything and everything: Focus your attention on what you really want.

Do you have anything to show?

At this point, you might have a chicken-and-egg problem. You need some basic promotional materials in order to compete for bookings, but in order to acquire most of those promo assets, you need to play out. At the very least, you need a bio and a halfway decent photo. (See Chapter 11 for guidance on writing that bio.) If you're just starting and those are all you have, be honest. Don't try to pretend you're experienced if you're not.

Starting from Scratch

If you are a brand-new act looking for your first bookings, start with low-risk targets. By "low-risk," I mean risk to the venue, not to you. You need to build up to getting booked into places where you must contribute to the draw or drive ticket sales. For now, look for places that have live music but it doesn't matter who is playing, like open mics, and also look for background or "wallpaper" gigs in places that have live music but it's not the focal point, like coffee shops, restaurants, and some hotel bars. With both of these types of gigs, open mic and background, you're not expected to attract attendees with your name or reputation. That's a responsibility you'll have in the future, but for now you're free of it.

Open-mic events will have a sign-up process, either in advance or at the venue ahead of the start time. The people in the audience will be a mix of friends of the performers, patrons of the establishment who just happen to be there, the other musicians who will be performing that night, and perhaps some music lovers who come out to discover and support the newest of the new talent in town. Even though these are probably the most sympathetic audiences you could ask for, it's fine if you're nervous. This is where you work it out.

In your networking, now's the time to start asking for introductions to people who book background live music and/or own or run those types of spaces: Coffee shop owners, restaurant and hotel managers, and event planners are a good start. It's also time to create at least one social media account if you haven't already and start developing the discipline of promoting yourself through it. You probably won't have many followers at first, and that's fine. For now, focus on advance-posting every show and tagging the venue in the event or post.

Don't limit yourself to places that already have live music. Why not go where there's no competition and develop your own market? If you know of a coffee shop that has a little corner where you could set up, talk to them about adding a set on a weekday evening or for Sunday brunch.

Places that don't already host music will probably not have a PA and microphone that you can use, so you'll need to borrow or buy them. Craigslist always has used music gear. That's a small inconvenience in exchange for the opportunity to be first on the scene.

Your very first booking pitch:

Ready to go for a wallpaper gig? Cool! It's finally time to reach out to strangers and ask them to hire you. This task has a reputation for sucking, but if you've read this book from the beginning, you know by now that it's not so bad when you have systems and the right attitude.

Write a starter template email, save it as a draft, and keep polishing it until it conveys your request and key info as efficiently and authentically as possible. There's an example of a booking pitch email for nontraditional venues in Chapter 14 to get you started.

While that email is simmering in draft form, start your booking contacts spreadsheet. (See Chapter 14 again for a sample.) This is where you'll begin tracking your booking outreach efforts. You might be amazed at how quickly it fills up.

Hit the internet and start identifying restaurants, coffee shops, and hotels to approach. Yelp can be a useful tool for this—not necessarily for the reviews, but for identifying establishments in the categories you're interested in by geographic location. Sometimes it's more efficient to find the names of these places on Yelp and jump from there to their websites than to try to identify them with a general browser search.

You're going to spend a lot of time on the "Contact Us" page of establishments' websites. Look at the staff listed there and their titles, and target the person who sounds most likely to have the privilege (or the chore, depending on how they view it) of hiring live music. These types of businesses are not primarily music venues, so they probably won't have an actual booking contact listed. You'll have to guess, and you'll probably speak with a lot of people who don't understand what you're asking for.

Start entering your prospective venues into your booking contacts spreadsheet. Even if they don't pan out, you want to remember that you tried them and what their response was, so list everyone. Once you have a target name and email address, use your template email to create a message specifically for this venue and this person. Yes, this means customizing each email, which is more work but also more likely to get you a response. Put the person's name in the subject line to make your note look less like spam (spammers do that too, but it might slightly increase the odds of your email being opened). If all you have is a general email address and no contact name, just open with "Hello!" and plan to follow up with a call or a visit.

Should you call or email first? Start with whichever you prefer; you'll do the other one when you follow up. If you call first, ask for your target person by name, and then ask him or her whether they book live music. If yes, the person might interview you right then or s/he might tell you to send an email for consideration. Mention in the email that you're following up on your phone call.

If you don't have a target person or if his or her calls are being screened by someone answering the phone, say you're calling about live music booking. Phrase it as a statement, not a question. Don't ask the screener whether they have live music—that makes it too easy for someone who doesn't know or care to just tell you no. The person still might reply that they don't have live music there, and at that point you can let it go, but at least you didn't set yourself up for an easy no.

If you don't get a reply to your first contact, wait at least a week and then call or send an email (whichever you didn't do initially) or stop in during the time of day you would like to play (but not in the middle of a meal rush) and ask for your contact person by name or simply the manager on duty. Update your spreadsheet with each step.

Speaking of stopping in, if you prefer that over email or calling as your first approach, there's nothing inherently wrong with it for this type of gig. It's more time-consuming and a bit more likely to be bothersome since you're asking for a person's attention right then vs. giving them a chance to answer you on their own timetable. But sometimes the organic, human approach works best. If you're already polished at networking, this might really appeal to you.

One strong caveat: Walk-ins are generally unwelcome at traditional live music venues (bars, nightclubs, etc.). The booker probably won't be there anyway, and if s/he is, s/he almost certainly doesn't want to take unscheduled meetings with unknown talent. For this type of venue, dropping in marks you as a newbie, not a go-getter.

How many of these establishments should you contact at the same time? Again, it's up to you, but with this type of starter or wallpaper gig, it would be reasonable to try just two or three at a time and follow through until you have an answer before reaching out to another batch. This type of booking is often a standing gig, meaning you'll have the job for more than one time, so you don't want to make yourself available to two dozen venues, get interest from more than you can accommodate, and have to turn some down. On the other hand, some advisors would tell you to go ahead and hit them all, and if you have to decline some, that will be good because it shows that you're in demand. If that approach resonates with you, go for it—just be sure to keep track of all of your contacts and conversations as you go.

Will they pay me?

Open mics generally do not pay unless they're run as a contest. There might even be a small entry fee. You might get some tips, though, or free coffee from the venue. Your purpose at these shows is not to get paid—it's to get experience in front of an audience and collect some promotional assets. This phase of your career, like the startup period of any business, will likely cost you more than it earns you.

Establishments that regularly book background music have a budget for it, or should. If they tell you that everyone plays there for free, or for tips only, consider the factors in your area—competitiveness, saturation of live music, number of other similar venues, level of tourism and nightlife, overall cost of living, etc.—and make an informed decision about whether you want to participate on their terms. They might even say that you have to pay them to play there. We'll discuss "pay-to-play" later in this chapter.

Whoo, you got booked!

When you get a wallpaper gig, your priorities are to be on time (better yet, be early), dress appropriately (ask in advance if they have "wardrobe preferences" for you to follow), set up quietly and efficiently, and play music that is pleasant and not distracting. These bookings are like being an extra in a movie. You're supposed to contribute to the scene without standing out from it. This can be frustrating when you're trying to be a star, but if you play your cards right, you won't have to do it this way for long.

There won't be a sound engineer to help you, so you will need to connect your instrument to their house PA and set your own volume (and mix, if there's a board). You might even have to set it all up yourself, using a cart of house gear that will be waiting for you when you get there. If you don't know how to do that, arrive extra-early and ask them to show you the first time.

It's worth noting that this type of gig is not just for newbies. Some artists find it to be a enjoyable, reliable source of steady income without all of the promotion and fanbase-building responsibilities.

What you really want from these starter gigs:

Two things: Practice and promo assets.

This is your chance to start developing your poise onstage and gaining good mistakes to learn from. You WANT things to go wrong with these gigs—that gives you the opportunity to work through glitches now, when the stakes are low, rather than later when more eyes and more demands are on you.

These gigs also give you the opportunity to start accumulating photos and videos for your electronic press kit (or EPK; more on this later), website, and social media. These are assets you need to get the attention of talent buyers for the "real" venues with paid gigs. Get a friend to come out and take photos of you performing, or, at an open mic, ask another of the musicians to take photos of you and then do the same for him or her. Even good cellphone photos are better than nothing.

Also get some video when you can. You can record it yourself on your own cellphone if you don't have someone to do it for you. At this point, the video is only for you to review, like a sports team watching the playback of their last game. Cringe all you want, but do it. This is how you learn. All of your mentors and heroes were once in your shoes.

If you start to generate some fans with these gigs, invite them to follow you on social media. Get their email addresses if you already have a mailing list and worthwhile things to say in an e-newsletter. If not, don't bother taking their email address to add to a list later. After a week or two, they probably won't remember who you are. Encourage them to follow you on social media instead, where you can invite them to sign up for your emails down the road.

Moving Up to "Real" Venues

When you've got enough performances under your belt, start looking for opportunities one rung up the ladder. You determine what is "enough performances" yourself: When you can get through a set without getting lost, when you have a feel for whether the audience is engaged, when you've had enough things go wrong that you can solve problems without losing your flow or panicking, when you have some good assets in your EPK—all of those are indicators that you're ready to move up.

In your networking, start asking for introductions to local musicians. Through those connections and musicians you already know, put the word out that you're looking for support slots. Finding reliable and at least moderately talented openers can be a challenge for bands who are putting together their own bill and for venues that need to put someone on the stage during their more lightly attended hours of operation.

Continue your booking pitch process, but now add some refinements that will make your emails more appropriate for communicating with people for whom booking/talent buying is their main job, not an occasional side task. The basic difference is concision: These people process hundreds of pitches a day, so you must give them the info they need, and only the info they need, in the most concise way possible. You'll find a another sample template email in Chapter 14. These folks will want examples of your sound and look. They're highly unlikely to book you without those assets, so get those links into your EPK.

The website Indie on the Move (www.indieonthemove.com) is an excellent resource for finding pertinent data on music venues, sometimes including crowdsourced information that the venue doesn't offer on its website or social media. There is ample starter info available at IOTM's free level, and the paid upgrade offers further data and administrative shortcuts that you might find worthwhile as you expand your number of gigs and geographic radius of touring. Between a venue's IOTM profile and website, most times you'll be able to find the contact info and booking pitch instructions you need.

What should I ask for?

Your "ask" to a talent buyer is similar to your "ask" in a networking meeting: Don't just tell them you're available for whatever—tell them specifically what you want. You might think this will come off as pushy or demanding, but it doesn't. It's like being in line at a busy lunch counter: Does the server welcome you asking for her recommendations? No. Would she like it if you told her to pick something for you? Hell no. She wants you to say what sandwich you want so she can either give it to you or tell you it's unavailable and move on.

The first considerations for every booking are standard yes-or-no questions: Do they book your type of act and do they have an opening in the calendar. If you try to sell them on your talent before those questions are answered, you'll just annoy them.

Further, those two questions are ones you can often answer yourself, and you are expected to do so. Look at the venue's website and IOTM listing to get an idea of the genres of music they book. If it's nothing like what you play, don't even ask. If it is, look at their online show calendar and find one or two blank dates, or timeslots before or after other bookings that look like they might be open for support, then ask for those specific dates and times in your pitch email.

As you're starting out, you'll probably have better luck going for off-nights rather than Fridays or Saturdays. A single Tuesday night could lead to a four-week Tuesday night residency, which could lead to a headlining Thursday or a weekend support slot. How well you keep up your end of promotion for every show and how professional you are as a performer will be noticed—not necessarily immediately rewarded, but noticed.

Don't ask about money in your initial email. Even if you're unwilling to play unless they pay you, get a reply before you even broach that subject.

Most of your emails will go unanswered. Even well-crafted pitches get buried or ignored, especially if they're from unknown artists but sometimes even when it's a booker you've worked with for years. Reread "S/he's Probably Just Busy" in Chapter 8 as many times as you need to until it's second nature. Send follow-ups at a reasonable pace (generally no more than once a week) and using empathetic language (see the follow-up email template in Chapter 14).

You're unlikely to get a rejection reply, but if you do, note that person in your spreadsheet as a booker who has his or her act together. Anyone who has time to answer you with a no is exceptionally organized or exceptionally attached to being courteous. If the rejection is for genre or some other unchangeable factor, cross that venue off your list. (Actually, I would move it to another sheet of dead ends rather than delete it entirely. Ya never know what might be useful down the road.) If the rejection is for date or something else that might be different next time, keep the venue in rotation to try again later.

When you do receive a reply, whether it's a rejection or an offer, it will likely be terse. Don't take that personally. An offer isn't going to be a certificate suitable for framing. More likely the entire reply will look something like this:

Fri. Jan. 20 8:30pm (30 min)—50% of door at $5—please confirm

If you get a reply with full sentences, consider it a bonus. ;) Understand that this brevity is no reflection of the talent buyers' manners, job satisfaction, or interest in your act—again, they're extraordinarily busy. You need to learn to read their shorthand and adapt to their communication style. Reply back to them at the same level of concision and with a quick thank-you:

[Act name] confirming for a 30 on Fri. Jan. 20 8:30pm. Will await details re: load-in/soundcheck. Thanks Joe!—[your name]

Add the date to your band calendar and set a task to follow up if you don't receive load-in and soundcheck times by one to two weeks prior. Then plug it into your promotion system (see Chapter 11). Your ability to draw is starting to matter, so promotion is now essential.

NOW will they pay me?

Maybe. If so, at this point it probably won't be much, but that's normal. Your objectives at this level are still to accumulate promotional assets and continue building your fanbase. In addition to those goals, you're also now building your reputation among talent buyers (including more veteran bands who get to choose their own openers), and part of that reputation is whether or not you play for free, demand a high guarantee, or take a more moderate approach to negotiation based on the circumstances of the gig. The number of attendees you can be expected to draw is generally the most important factor that talent buyers consider, and that number is what both you and they will use to negotiate the amount and nature of your pay (whether bar split, door split, flat guarantee, or a combination of these). When you don't yet have a reliable draw, your promotion work for past shows (in evidence online and through the grapevine) can be the factor that convinces a booker to take a chance on you.

Debate rages over whether musicians should play for free, a.k.a. for "exposure." Sometimes it's a value, particularly if you're an excellent networker and there are people there worth networking with; other times it's just exploitation. Money isn't the only worthwhile form of compensation—sometimes the opportunity to be seen by key people is worth far more than a cut of the bar or even a large guarantee—but to benefit from exposure gigs, you have to be especially strong in your business operations. Like everything else, make an informed choice.

Pay-to-play is another booking model to be aware of. This one is mostly condemned by advocates of indie musicians because it so often results in a bad deal for the artist. Pay-to-play arrangements require you to put up money in order to be booked. It might be a fee paid to the promoter or it might be a number of tickets you're required to buy that you can then resell (in theory) to recoup your upfront cost. The objection to this model as expressed by artist advocates is that it puts all the risk on the artist and none on the promoter or venue. The promoter and venue then have very little motivation to spend money on promoting the show because they've already gotten paid, regardless of whether anyone comes out to see the performances. Another objection is that these bills (usually showcases with many acts in very short sets) are not assembled based on talent, ability, or stage readiness. If you pay, you're booked, even if you've never been onstage. Because there is no natural development process in this type of booking, it's common for artists to perform poorly, which not only torpedoes their budding confidence but also turns off any legitimate talent scouts or fans who happen to be in attendance. The general consensus is that pay-to-play sets you up to fail both creatively and financially.

Settlement:

When you do start getting paid gigs, don't forget to collect your pay (i.e. "settle" the show) before you leave. Every band has a settlement horror story, so you probably will too, eventually. But if you're organized, you can at least prevent self-inflicted problems like miscalculating the payout, forgetting to empty the tip jar, having the merch cash walk off, or failing to get the venue payment because everyone in the band thought someone else did it.

Decide in advance who in the band is responsible for settling and make sure that person has the original agreement email available for reference. Be prepared to do a cash count with the venue manager (so if doing math under pressure makes you nervous, you might not be the best choice for the task), and anticipate deductions for guest-list spots and the band's food or bar tab if they weren't part of the deal. Always ask what the door count was for your records, even if that wasn't your payment basis: You need to track your draw for ongoing booking pitches and to monitor your growth over time.

Saturation or scarcity?

These are two different strategies for performing in your local market. Either way can work, but you should make an intentional choice about them, not simply bounce between them due to inconsistent booking effort. In general, if you want to play a city's higher capacity rooms, you'll have an easier time filling them if you play fewer shows in that city. This is the scarcity approach: If you only do a few shows a year, your fans will be more motivated to come to most or all of them because you're not easily accessible.

However, for scarcity to work, you need to have a well-established fanbase and conduct intense promotion of each show to make sure everyone knows about it.

Saturation, on the other hand, is when you play out so often that your fans will have no trouble seeing you in any given week. Residencies, in which you have a standing gig at a venue on the same night each week, fit into this strategy, and the effect is amplified if you play elsewhere in town on other nights. Saturation is often the way to go when your focus is building your fanbase and you're able to play venues for which high draw generated directly by you is not the top priority—for example, a lounge or restaurant that promotes its upcoming acts by name (so it's not strictly a background gig), but it has a built-in crowd due to its own popularity. The jackpot is when your residency becomes the place to be every week and you start to draw not only large audiences but also media attention as the hot new act in town.

This consideration of scarcity vs. saturation is an example of the importance of a long-term plan for your music career. If you simply start fishing for bookings anywhere you can get them with no attention to how frequently you're playing, you miss the opportunity to control the pace of your growth and to bring in and retain fans in a steady, sustainable, organized way.

Self-producing shows:

The most straightforward way to make sure you get booked is to book yourself. If you're highly organized, have a good number of musicians among your contacts, and have the funds to take on the initial risk of renting a venue and promoting a multi-act show, you can create your own gig. Take a look at the checklist for self-producing shows in Chapter 14.

Another self-booking avenue is online shows. More elaborate than a spontaneous social media live-stream, you can plan, promote, and sell tickets to broadcasts of your performances—even simple acoustic sets in your living room. Check out platforms like Concert Window and YouTube's live function to see how it's done, and read more about live-streaming in Chapter 11: Promotion.

Private events:

If your act is a fit for corporate events, weddings, and other private parties (i.e. if your music is fun, danceable, and appealing to a broad audience, and you're willing to play mostly covers), these constitute another potential booking opportunity for you. You'll learn about these events primarily from fans who see your public shows and through your networking efforts.

The booking process is very different for these events compared to typical club gigs. You might be approached by an event planner, but often the client will hire you directly. It is recommended that you have a performance agreement to present to the client for these shows; in contrast, club bookings typically have no written contract. Private events tend to pay far better than club bookings which for many bands eases the pain of going back to the wallpaper/cover songs format. Do your research to determine what you should charge for private events and to learn what elements you should include in your performance agreement.

Expanding Your Horizons

If you choose to seek out bookings at larger-capacity rooms and with festivals or venues beyond your city, the booking outreach and promotion steps might become more complex but the processes will stay essentially the same. You'll need to keep your EPK complete and fresh, adding recordings, videos, media coverage, and other assets as you acquire them, and you'll need to hold sustained focus on maintaining and growing your fanbase. The systems and tools you've honed from the beginning will serve you well as the admin components of your career get more involved, the opportunities become more lucrative, and mistakes become more problematic.

Overnights are a significant milestone. Even if you're just doing two shows with one overnight in between, the logistical complexity skyrockets when you can't run back home for a forgotten piece of gear and you have to handle all of your grooming and dressing out of a bag in a hotel or a friend's guest room. When you graduate to multi-night touring, you will have to be able to replicate all of your core life functions on the road: Not just casual survival like on vacation, not just a subset of working as with a week at a business conference, but actually living your life, running your business, and performing your act while physically disconnected from all of the resources, comforts, and familiar routines of your home base. You know what I suggest: Checklists, schedules, spreadsheets, and procedural safeties. You'll find some examples of tools for touring in Chapter 14.

Tour routing: Big rocks first

Remember the Big Rocks First analogy from Chapter 1? It's a great strategy for making sure the most important time commitments get into your calendar first, and it's also the recommended strategy for booking a tour. The big rocks in this case are anchor shows: The gigs that will be the most lucrative. These might be private events for which the advance deposit is funding a large portion of the tour, or club dates with solid guarantees, or festival slots ahead of which you can add media appearances and day shows. Once you have one or more anchors booked (i.e. the big rocks are in the pitcher), you begin the game of filling in the spaces in between (pouring the pebbles, sand, and water into the gaps around the big rocks). These will be smaller club dates on weeknights, radio or TV in-studios, record store day shows, house concerts, afternoon or evening shows on college campuses, secret pop-up shows, scheduled live-stream acoustic sets or q&a with the band from cool locations along the route, and any other clever way you can think of to squeeze in a performance, appearance, or social media event.

The challenge is to pack in as much useful activity as you can without burning yourselves out and to do it all on a route that is as efficient as possible, with minimal wasted miles. You might also need to turn a profit in order to consider it a successful tour; that's up to you and your business structure. The question of whether it's worthwhile to tour for market development even if it costs you money is another debate you can read all about on the interwebs.

Who's going with you?

Is the whole band going on the road, or just a subset? Will you play stripped-down sets with those members, or will you hire subs who are based in each city? What about taking locals from your town who are willing to tour as subs for bandmembers who aren't? These questions need to be settled before you start booking a tour. It won't work to ask each member gig by gig. Filling a tour route is even more hellish than booking locally because so many more contingencies are at play: Every date and pitch has an if/then relationship with every other one, rather than the relatively simple yes/no of one-off local shows. Your booker needs to be able to respond to offers immediately without having to check with the band.

Before you start asking for commitments from players to join the tour, and before you commit to them, you'll need to draft a budget and figure out how many others you can afford to take along. See the Tour Budget Worksheet in Chapter 14 for a start on working out these numbers.

How much will it cost?

This is not a simple or easy question to answer. If you absolutely cannot afford to lose money on a tour, you will have to plan very carefully to keep expenses down and book skillfully to secure guarantees at almost all of your stops--a tall order for an unknown band but not impossible.

One of your biggest expenses will be paying your musicians (and they might want to be paid more than usual because they'll be away from their day jobs). This might sound cold, but there is a point at which additional bodies on the road become purely an expense: If you have three horns in your full-band show, you have to ask the hard question of whether they contribute enough to your draw and therefore to the tour's revenue to justify the cost of a larger van, additional motel rooms, and additional paychecks. The unpleasant but honest answer might be that one horn will suffice. Bottom line: Perhaps the only realistic way for you to tour is with just a subset of your bandmembers.

Plan for disaster:

What will you do if you have an emergency expense on the road? Are you budgeting for the additional roadside assistance insurance in your van rental? If you're taking personal vehicles, do you have AAA or the equivalent, and does it apply outside of your normal travel area? Do you have theft insurance for your gear? In the back of your mind, are you counting on a credit card or a call to Mom and Dad as your safety net? Talk about these things. If no one in the band has any sort of financial backup, think hard about whether it's safe to head out into the unknown. A few years ago, my previously 100% reliable SUV broke down on a blazing summer day in the Texas desert while towing a trailer with band gear. The tow truck driver extorted us for $300 for a 5-mile tow to the closest truck stop, where we waited the rest of the day for my husband to drive 7 hours with a car-hauler to rescue us. What if we had been farther away? What if I weren't married to a mechanic who knew what to do and had the ability to do it? How would we have gotten ourselves, the gear, and the rented trailer back? No idea. Make sure you have a reliable safety net.

Working from the road:

When you go on tour, your family and friends might think you're getting a paid vacation and all you have to do is play a show once a night. Wrong ... so wrong. Touring is not vacation, paid or otherwise, and the administrative work doesn't pause itself until you get back. Almost everything you need to do on the biz side these days can be done remotely, which means it can be done from the road and you will be expected to do it, even on crappy motel wifi. You can't be unreachable or hide behind a vacation email autoresponder.

This underscores the importance of having a good laptop and reliable digital systems (see Chapter 13). You should have all of your tools and systems down cold before you take them on the road, because everything's harder and more likely to fail out there. Don't make unnecessary changes or additions to your processes right before a tour. It's disorienting enough trying to work in stolen moments and strange locations—you'll be grateful for anything familiar and easy.

Here are more hard-earned organizational hints to help you prevent major and minor touring disasters:

- Take printed directions when you're driving an unfamiliar route. Many areas still have no cellphone or GPS service, and it's not just places you're unlikely to go: In West Texas, for example, cell coverage drops between some of the cities of the Viva Big Bend festival and it's completely nonexistent at Utopiafest (something the producers consider a selling point). If you're in more than one vehicle, make sure everyone has a printed copy of the directions, plus the exact address of the next venue and hotel and contact numbers for both. If you're leaving at different times, know which freeways each vehicle will be taking. Agree that if anyone loses cell connectivity, you will meet at a specified place (e.g. the venue or hotel).

- If you use a cloud-based file storage system, save copies of your key documents to your hard drive so you can access them without internet connectivity. Test this before you head out. If you're going to discover that your word processing and spreadsheet apps only work while you're connected to the internet, even if you stored your files locally, you don't want to make that discovery hours before departure.

- Carry emergency cash in case your bank cards don't work at some remote gas station. Make sure you know how to transfer funds from your phone, via app or call.

- Confirm that you have adequate insurance coverage if your gear is stolen. If you don't, load it all into the motel with you each night or have someone sleep in the van to guard it. Talk about this in advance so it's not an unwelcome surprise to anyone.

- If the tour is long enough to require doing laundry, plan in advance where and when you will do it. Bring detergent and fabric softener from home.

- Designate (beg, bribe) someone back home to be on call for you if something happens that you can't resolve easily or at all from the road. Equip the person in advance with whatever logins and account numbers s/he might need. For example, if you find out on the way to the venue that tomorrow night's lodging fell through, hit up your back-home helper to find and book you a replacement.

Thoughts to Ponder on Booking & Touring

Know the law about booking agents:

In many states, booking agents are required to be licensed, even if they're working exclusively for your band and perhaps in a capacity such as manager. It's up to you to decide whether to work only with a licensed one. Do some research about the law in your state, read the debates about pros and cons of using unlicensed agents, and make an informed choice.

The nightmare of the ghosted talent buyer:

This does happen: You get confirmed for a gig (or think it's confirmed anyway) with nothing more than the date and set time, and then the booker stops responding to you. The date approaches and you have no info on load-in, soundcheck, or pay. The show isn't listed on the venue's calendar or social media. What do you do?

You actually have a lot of options: Call the venue's main phone and keep calling until someone answers. Send a private message to their Facebook page (politely) asking for an update. Stop in and ask for a manager's help. Reach out to the band listed on their calendar as most recently playing there and ask if they have a better venue contact or any intel on what's going on. Sooner or later somebody will clue you in. What you should NOT do is assume it's a no-go, or, conversely, trust that everything's OK and they'll get you the info eventually, ignore the fact that they're not advertising your show at all, or guess that load-in is probably an hour before and just show up then. It's not inappropriate to politely and persistently ask for the support and information you need.

No whining:

Don't second-guess your band's booker, whether it's a bandmember or an outside agent. Booking is a complicated job with multiple moving parts. It requires compromises and quick decisions which often must be made with incomplete information. Don't make it harder with your 20/20 hindsight. If your booker tells you soundcheck is 4pm for a 9pm show, go ahead and ask why so early if you're curious, but don't push him or her to try to change it. Yes, it's no fun to sit around for 5 hours before you play. Nobody's happy about it, but sometimes that's just the way it is. Complaining about it won't win you any points with your booker or the talent buyer.

Watch for the advance:

Some bookings will be followed by one or more informational emails and requests or instructions regarding promotion and logistics. This process is referred to as "advancing" and the materials sent are advances. It is imperative that you do not miss or lose these emails and that you follow all instructions and respond to every request. You might be asked to advance your stage plot and inputs list to the venue or event contact or directly to the sound engineer to prepare for your performance. You might also be asked or even required to send your PR photos, social media links, and other basic promo assets. Biscuits & Blues in San Francisco provides detailed guidance and abundant promo support for bands that follow their instructions. (Even if you don't receive a request, these are items that you would do well to send ahead anyway.) Advances will often contain small details that you need to comply with—things like how to obtain parking passes or security clearance, which social media handles to use when you tag the show, and what to do with gear cases after you've loaded in. This is other people's attempts at being organized—don't be the one who messes them up.

Radius expectations:

If you have two shows booked within a short timeframe and within the same market, you might enrage either or both of the talent buyers who gave you those shows. Some venues and bookers impose a "radius" for their acts, meaning you are not allowed to play another promoted public show within a certain number of miles and days from their show. Radius clauses are typical in festival contracts, but even clubs that don't use contracts will often expect you to know better than to step on your own draw at their show by promoting another one at the club down the street within the same week or two. Notice how this gets complicated if you're using the saturation approach discussed previously.

Habits that support repeat bookings:

Be on time or early. Be nice to everyone, even the door guy who yelled at you and the sound gal who snapped at you. Tag and thank the venue in before, during, and after posts. Take crowd photos that make the place look attractive and full. Start and end on time. Keep track of compliments from staff and casually mention them in conversations with management or the booker the next time around. Tip the bar staff even if free drinks are part of your deal. Pick up after yourself in the green room, at the merch area, and on the stage as you load out. Follow the posted rules. Stay sober. Have zero tolerance for drama at the venue among bandmembers, significant others, and anyone else associated with you. Thank the venue from the stage, remind the audience to drink/eat/whatever else makes the venue money, and thank the staff again as you're leaving. Load out efficiently and get out of their way so they can close up and go home.

You don't have to tour:

You get to run your business your way. That's the beauty of self-employment. You don't have to tour to be a legitimate working musician. If you love playing live but hate travel, or want to be home every night to tuck your kids in, or much prefer growing your non-local audience through live-streaming rather than live-in-person, build your career around that. You're the boss of you.

CHAPTER 10:
RECORDING & DISTRIBUTION

Reminder: I'm an organizer, not a musician. I'm not going to presume to tell you how to make your music. Everything in this chapter (and in the rest of the book) is about the *organizational processes around* the making of your music.

Sometimes your org choices might impact or be impacted by creative choices, and you'll need to sort those out yourself, wearing both hats. I can tell you that having a chronically late player is disruptive to the band's processes and will cost you time, money, and possibly opportunity, but only you can decide if that player's creative contribution is worth the cost.

With that said, let's look at some of the choices you can anticipate ahead of recording and distributing your music. Note that these questions might or might not be in contingency order: You may have initial preferences with all of these, but your funding success will likely end up calling the shots.

Self-, Band-, or Crowdfunded?

If you already have the money saved for your next (or first) round of recording, you'll have an easier time making the rest of your decisions because you know your overall budget. However, a lot of artists and bands launch into recording projects before they have all of the money they'll need and hope to fill in with ongoing band revenue, a successful crowdfunding campaign, perhaps some less-than-ideal credit card usage, or, last resort, a heartfelt call to the folks back home.

Whichever way you're doing it, spell it all out before you start any work. Now is not the time to say, "We'll figure it out," and just leave it at that. It might be that you think it's obvious that every bandmember will need to chip in, but turns out they're unwilling or unable. Clarifying your financial realities will reveal your options going forward.

Whether or not they chip in to cover the cost of recording, bandmembers will be "paying" in another way: With their time. They will have to be available for as many hours as they're needed, even if this means multiple days off work or away from other commitments. Again, don't simply assume that this is understood and will be done: Discuss it.

DIY or Hired Out?

How times have changed: If you want to, and if you have the baseline skills and equipment, you can make and distribute a pro-level recording entirely by yourself. Austin's godfather of hip-hop, Terrany Johnson, does it all the time, not just for sale to consumers but also for sync licensing, where technical quality is arguably even more important. This was certainly not an option a generation ago, back when labels ruled the industry. Now the question isn't whether you can or can't do it yourself. The question is, which resource do you want to use as payment: Money or time?

The more money you have, the more options you have. You can buy the services the project needs much more quickly and reliably with money (paying pros) than with time (learning to do it at pro-level). And you don't have to outsource every aspect of the project: You can still choose to do some things yourself, even if you could afford to pay for them. Maybe you're experienced enough to self-produce and you have a solid home studio, but you need someone to engineer and mix for you. Maybe you feel comfortable with everything except mastering. Or maybe you could do it all yourself but you just don't want to. It comes down to that fundamental question of which is more valuable to you in this context: money or time.

Keep in mind that a high price doesn't guarantee great results. The most expensive producers and studios are not necessarily the best for getting the sound you want. It could very well be that you already know a local who does excellent mixing (looking at you, Michael Ingber in Austin, TX). The same is true of studio musicians: Sometimes the most expensive hired guns are the best because they show up on time, well-rehearsed, and do their job in one take. Other times, their high fee is buying you their notoriety, not any sort of work ethic. If you let go of the idea that you must have famous names on your project, you'll open up a much broader array of options.

Be careful not to end up paying in both money AND time. Just as a high price doesn't guarantee a great-sounding product, it also doesn't guarantee a brisk work pace. Even if you're paying the person a flat project fee instead of an hourly rate, a slow-moving engineer or player will cost you money elsewhere in the project. In fact, sometimes the more sought after the person is, the slower he or she will work. From an organizational perspective, if their skill level is equivalent, the more efficient worker is the better choice.

Your band or studio players?

Depending on your existing relational dynamics, this could be a non-issue for your band or it could be a massive fight-starter. It's not uncommon for bands to record with different players than they have in their live shows. There's nothing inherently wrong with it, either—some players shine in the studio, some shine onstage, and it makes sense to go with those who will create the best product in each realm. But if this hasn't already been discussed and understood with your core bandmembers, they will likely assume they're going to be included on the recording and when they learn otherwise, it probably won't be pretty.

Here again, you'll have to wear both the admin and the creative hat and decide whether replacing a bandmember in the studio will be worth it. If you choose to keep the peace and skip the hired gun, plan ahead to compensate for the shortcomings that made you consider excluding that bandmember.

It's a lot to think about. Jimmy George, guitarist, producer/engineer, and owner of The Roost Recording Studios in Manchaca, TX, observes, "There can be a thin line between striving towards a level of technical performance perfection in production vs. the organic nature that happens in playing together as a band live without a click track in order to fully capture the unrestricted synergy. A great performance can outweigh technical deficiencies, for example if a guitar or vocal is slightly out of pitch or a moment slightly off-tempo, but the overall performance is authentic and moving. There are also great moments that can come from mistakes or working around limitations within a song's structure. Thinking outside the box has its merits. That said, there is still a base level of proficiency that each bandmember has to bring to the performance."

If you're working with an outside producer who isn't closely familiar with each member, give him or her a heads-up about the potential problem with this player. If it's a matter of skill, will extra rehearsal help? Or should his or her parts simply be made less challenging? If you're doing group takes in a live room, this weak link will be much more of a liability than if you're multi-tracking individually and his or her parts can be more easily fixed in post or even deleted. Even if everyone is mic'ed separately in the group take, the weak player's flubs can distract the other players and create a domino effect of underperformance.

If it's a problem of cooperation or time management, what safeties can you put in place to reduce the risk of this member disrupting sessions and throwing the project off-track? Do you need to trick him or her into being on time by lying about the start time? Do you need to keep this member separated from another player that s/he tends to fight with? Does this person need extra time, attention, or solitude to get into the right frame of mind? If any of these accommodations need to be made and are worth it to you, prepare for them in advance. And just in case worse comes to worst, keep that hired gun on speed dial.

Albums, EPs, or Singles?

This is both a tactical and a creative decision. Before you make this choice, read up on what types of recordings are currently selling the best, in general and in your genre, and in both physical and digital formats. Consider what you anticipate your fans will want, but also consider what will be most satisfying to you as an artist. Then balance those considerations within the reality of your budgets of both money and time.

We've talked about the advantages of being proactive vs. reactive in other contexts (notably in how you decide what to do each day), and that advantage applies here as well. Whichever choice you make, whether to release your music in the large batch of an album, the small batch of an EP, or the individual serving of a single, you'll have the most options and the least stress if you're making this choice because it's what you really want, both tactically and creatively, not because you have to compromise due to disorganization. If you started recording with the intention of putting out an album but you ended up with an EP or a single because you ran out of time or money, that's not a strategic decision—that's settling. You don't need that kind of discouragement.

Physical Media or Digital Only?

Again, this is both a tactical and a creative decision which calls for research, and it should be decided before you start recording. Consider what's standard in your genre now. Do you already have a fanbase, and do they expect CDs or do they purchase and listen to digital almost exclusively? Are you familiar with the costs and options of CD printing plants vs. print-on-demand services which don't require an upfront bulk purchase? Would it be weird not to have CDs at your merch table, or is traditional live performance not a major part of your strategy?

Some engineering decisions are made based on what the final medium will be, so educate yourself on topics like lossiness and the differences between .MP3 and .WAV. And before you hop on the vinyl, ahem, bandwagon, even more research is in order before you can make an informed decision. First ask yourself whether you're considering vinyl as a strategic move or, honestly, just because you love vinyl and want to hear yourself on it. If that's your reason, think hard about whether it will be a rational business decision. Do you understand the differences in engineering that make vinyl truly "vinyl" vs. a vinyl cut of a digital recording? Do you know the limitations of this medium? Are you prepared to adjust your recording process and/or spring for additional mastering to accommodate the special needs of vinyl vs. CD? Do you have the budget to bulk-order vinyl and the proper space to store your backstock? If your music is nuanced enough to be enhanced by the listening experience of vinyl and you can absorb the expense, special storage, and additional merch transport load, or if your fans are already so into vinyl that you know the hassle will be worth it, then vinyl makes business sense. If not, it will be a gimmick and a merch expense that will take you a long time to recoup.

Brick-by-Brick or Song-a-Day?

This is very much an organizational question, but the decision depends heavily on your and your players' creative outlook, abilities, and preferences. This topic deserves an in-depth discussion with your engineer well before recording begins, so that you can choose the best approach for yourself and your project, and also to ensure that everyone involved is ready to work in the same way and understands why you've chosen this approach.

To help you see this in organizational terms, imagine organizing everything in your home. You have two basic ways to do it: By category or by room. If you go by category, you'll organize all of the clothing in each room, then all of the books, all of the tools, and so on. This is like recording in the method known as "brick-by-brick": Completing one instrument's parts for all of the songs on the album or EP, then moving on to the next instrument.

In the second option for organizing your home, if you go by room, you'll organize to completion each category of things in one room, then repeat that process in the next room, and the next room, and so on. This is like recording song-by-song, more often referred to as "song-a-day."

It's important to know that, either way, there will likely be some doubling back and revising of earlier work based on new discoveries. You can prevent most of this in pre-production, but you don't want to be so rigid about the rules that you bypass inspiration when it strikes mid-stream. In the categorical or brick-by-brick approach, you might get through the rhythm parts for all of the songs and move on to guitars, only to realize there's something you need to change about bass in one or more songs. In the song-a-day approach, you might have used a cool vocal technique on the first song, but when you get to the fourth song you realize that technique would be even more impactful there. You don't want to overuse it by having it on both songs, but now you really want it on this one, so you go back and change the first song.

When weighing brick-by-brick vs. song-a-day, understand that neither method is inherently superior, but one is likely a better fit for you than the other. Make an informed decision about this in consultation with your players, your producer if you have a separate one, and your engineer.

Pre-Production: Preparing to Record

This is where it gets super-exciting for organizing nerds. When you're getting ready to head into the studio, there is so much you can do in advance to set yourself up for success. If you treat this period as a sub-project of its own, with its own tasks and timeline, all leading up to the whirlwind performance of the recording sessions, you'll be much more likely to get the results you want, on time and within budget.

Pre-pro is to recording what rehearsal is to performing: It's the time you take to prepare yourself to do your very best under pressure. You have both creative and administrative tasks to complete during the pre-production stage, many of which will be done concurrently. I've listed some for you in a checklist in Chapter 14.

First, make sure you're starting this process early enough. I can't tell you how much time you'll need because so much depends on your development as a band and the complexity of the recording project, but this much is certain: If you're recording eight songs and you're starting pre-pro a week before the first session, you are already desperately behind.

Distribution Choices

If this is your first recording and/or you don't already have distribution channels set up, choose them or at least research them thoroughly and pick your finalists before you record. As with your choices about physical and digital media, there might be decisions you'll make in the budgeting or mechanics of the recording and production process that will affect your distro choices and vice versa.

As a DIY artist, your potential digital reach is broader than your physical, although distributors are making physical distro more accessible for indie artists. You have this in common with self-published authors, some of whom have become successful and well-known purely through their Kindle sales and without a physical presence in bookstores. It will probably make sense for you to focus the bulk of your energy on choosing your digital distribution platforms, but don't entirely discount the idea of having your CDs or vinyl in brick-and-mortar record stores.

Digital distributors such as Tunecore, CD Baby, ReverbNation, and DistroKid make your music available for download or streaming in dozens (and dozens) of online stores and platforms. You keep all ownership and copyrights for your music, and you pay the distributor a fee or percentage of sales for being your online merch vendor. You have quite a few distribution companies to choose from, and many of them offer other services to indie artists, so you might already be working with one or more of them in a different capacity. It would be tempting to simply add on distribution as a bundled service with a company you already know, but take the time to research all of them. Their fee and commission structures vary, as do the features they offer. Some can also serve as your publisher and sync licensing representative, which does get into potential sharing of your ownership stake—not necessarily bad, but you definitely want to understand what you're agreeing to. Bottom line: Choosing your distributor is a decision you don't want to make impulsively or lightly.

Some digital companies also offer physical distribution or a hybrid called "print on demand." Amazon.com, for example, enables you to sell physical CDs which are pressed, packaged, and shipped to the buyer as they are ordered, even just one at a time. As of this writing, for example, you could sell directly through Amazon's CreateSpace service or choose a distributor that includes Amazon among the many stores it places your music in.

Don't forget the most basic, grass-roots methods for physical distribution: Your merch table at shows, your website, and independent record stores. Each requires you to allocate time and storage space. Selling merch at your shows means schlepping merch to your shows and getting someone to work the table (see Chapters 11 and 14); selling directly through your website requires watching for and fulfilling incoming orders; and selling in record stores means persuading them to stock your music and keeping in touch to receive your earnings and replenish their supply of your items. All three require you to pre-purchase a quantity of your items and store them in climate-controlled safety.

Thoughts to Ponder on Recording & Distribution

Plan PR before setting a date:

Give some thought to how you're going to promote this release before you promise that it will be out on a certain date. If there's any chance at all that you might use a PR rep, flesh out your plans with him or her before you settle on a date. Even without professional representation, you might stumble into a great promotional opportunity that would require a worthwhile delay, so have that plan close to finished before you set your release date in stone.

Manage expectations for the studio:

Will players be using only their own instruments or also some house ones? Will supplies like strings, picks, and drumsticks be available? Will there be anyone other than the band and engineers there, such as photographers, videographers, interns, friends, kids, etc.? Are there any little corners or rooms to go to for solitude, either to warm up or just to chill? What's the parking situation? What about crime in the area? Anything you can anticipate and prepare for will make it that much easier to get oriented and get down to work.

Pack a lunch:

Or dinner, and also snacks, drinks, ibuprofen, Tums, throat spray, Band-Aids, cigarettes, and any other small comforts and conveniences that will prevent having to run out for stuff while the studio clock is ticking.

Consign wherever you tour:

Just as you do pre-promotion ahead of each tour stop, you can also do a bit of "after-promotion" by visiting the town's indie record store and asking them to stock your CDs. Stores generally have a consignment model through which they pre-purchase a small quantity of your items at their consignment price (similar to buying wholesale), sell them at retail, and pay you a portion of the profit. It's on you to stay in touch with them to collect your profits and send them more inventory if they sell out.

CHAPTER 11:

PROMOTION

Q: If a band plays in the forest and there's no one there to hear them, do they make a sound?
A: It doesn't matter.

●

If you want to make a career out of music, you have to promote yourself.

As a recording artist, it's your job to get people to buy your songs. If you perform live, it's on you to drive attendance to your shows. As a studio musician and/or side player, you have to position yourself to be top-of-mind when bands are looking for someone to play what you play for a gig or a session. Even if you're strictly a songwriter, you still have to promote yourself to get connected with the artists who will record and perform the songs you've written.

Defining Your Brand

In addition to knowing what your product is before you can sell it, you need to decide in advance what it's going to look like. People will recognize you not just for the named elements of your act (your band name, songs, albums, etc.) but also according to elements like your logo, color scheme, promotional "voice," and projected personality of your act. It's good strategy to choose these identifiable elements with intention early on, keeping in mind that you are free to change them over time but that every change can cause brand confusion for fans, media, and industry contacts.

Conveying a consistent branding message gives the impression that you are a professional working with a plan. Deciding these elements in advance also streamlines your promotional activities and makes it easier to delegate: When you have a defined set of branding elements such as logo, colors, fonts, and personality, you can more easily give parameters to someone helping you design show posters, for example.

Project vs. Event Promotion

You have two basic promo jobs: Promoting each of your events and promoting your project (your band, or yourself if you're solo). This requires you to simultaneously focus on both the ongoing big picture and the details of the present and near future—the macro vs. micro focus we talked about earlier. It's a fine example of why time management and project management are critical skills for every indie musician.

It's easy to get overwhelmed with the day-to-day tasks of upcoming shows and neglect important-but-not-urgent aspects of promotion, like relationship-building and EPK updates. That's because the trajectory of your career is always more nebulous than the next event. The project is what you squint at on the horizon; the event is the exit you need to take in half a mile. When you get into a busy period of show after show, stop after stop on the route either figuratively or literally, a solid long-term plan frees you to blindly follow the route you've mapped for yourself without having to zoom out and reconsider it unless something goes dramatically awry. Once there's a break in the action—the end of the tour, the completion of the funding campaign, delivery of the album for mastering, or even just a night off—that's when you go back to the big-picture view and recalibrate if necessary.

Project promotion:

This is the level of promotion that derives from your big-picture strategic decisions and enriches your event promotion. You need to be clear on your overall direction, band structure, and branding in order to promote the project effectively. Event promotion can be done without settled answers to those questions—plenty of people throw together a poster and put on a show—but unless that show is meant to be a one-off special event, it's not part of an organized career strategy and it's not moving the needle on any master plan. It can even backfire and create new problems.

Remember in Chapter 1 when we talked about urgent vs. important? The elements of project promotion are usually important but not urgent. They generally don't have deadlines. It's things like starting and maintaining your website and social media accounts, building your EPK and keeping it current, growing your live photo and video library with occasional new entries, amassing an expanding email list with ongoing signups at shows and online, and keeping a running list of media outlets to approach with appropriate frequency. These are all promotional elements that get back-burnered in the craziness of the everyday, but in hindsight, you'll regret not getting around to them.

Consider this situation: You enter a battle of the bands and you win. A couple dozen people introduce themselves after the show and express interest in your band from various angles. You go home with a pocketful of business cards. What will you do with each of those contacts? If you have a strategy already mapped out, you'll recognize what a promotional goldmine this is, immediately plan your responses, and contact each of them while the lead is still warm:

- TV reporter, books live weekday morning performances: Get her to schedule us ASAP to tie in the news of the win. Add to band calendar and alert everyone to take the morning off from day jobs. Remember to mention the upcoming album on-air. When performance goes well, get her to book us for six months out to promote the new album & give them the exclusive premiere of a new song. Also look up other stations and see if they do live music spots.
- Corporate guy from out of town, wants us for a private event in their city: Agree on date ASAP. Block off gig plus travel days in band calendar pending receipt of signed contract. Negotiate guarantee plus travel and lodging reimbursement. Get half upfront with signed contract. Change dates in band cal from tentative to confirmed. Reserve backline rental in their town. Book flights and hotel. When event goes well, get contact to introduce us to his colleagues at different companies, and/or same company in other divisions.
- Newspaper reporter, running a news story on the win and wants a follow-up feature next week: Email him the publicity photo, social links, bandmembers' names/instruments, and a quote about how stoked we are to have won. Schedule

interview and photos for first half-hour of next rehearsal. Share the news story as soon as it comes out & boost the post for a week according to budget. Get publication date for feature & tease on social media. Share feature when published on first day, again a week later, again a month later. Add reporter to contact list for album promo.

- Videographer, says he does music videos, wants to work with us: Email now & tell him we'll keep him in mind for next album release. Save rest of contact info. Schedule to hit him up for a price quote in about three months, during album promo planning.
- Music supervisor, loved "Crazy Song," wants to submit it for a TV show she's working on, needs the .WAVs with and without vocals immediately: Email her tonight for contract specs. If agreeable send the files.
- Studio owner, wants us to record at his place: Email him that we already have a studio and producer for the next album but would like to come visit. Add him to networking contacts.
- Booker from tonight's venue, offered us a 4-week weeknight residency: Check their online calendar & try for Mondays or Thursdays to avoid rehearsal and Joey's work schedule. Start no sooner than 2 weeks from now to give time to promote but no later than a month to ride the hype of the contest win. Confirm pay agreement and backline situation. Get their house marketing rep's name to coordinate promo. Once they see residency is going well, start asking about a Friday or Saturday night.

All of these responses can happen immediately because a) you've taken responsibility for band communication and made up your mind to stay on top of it; b) parameters like bandmember availability, minimum acceptable pay, rehearsal schedule, and brand messaging have already been decided; and c) you already have tools including social media channels, a shared band calendar, EPK, publicity photo, private event booking contract template, and all of your recordings in both .WAV and .MP3 and both with and without vocals for sync licensing.

That's what it looks like to have your act together. How would it look if you didn't?

- TV reporter: By the time you get everyone to agree on a date and find a sub for the member who refuses to take time off work, too much time has passed and your Battle of the Bands win is no longer newsworthy. She tells you to try her back for the album release.
- Corporate guy: You make an agreement by email with no contract and no deposit. You take the amount they offer because it sounds like a lot, but after you pay for travel and lodging, you realize you lost money on the deal. The band is pissed and doesn't want to do any more out-of-town private events.
- Newspaper reporter: Does a short news story with a photo he took at the show. For the feature, interviews just you by phone because you can't get everyone together in person. Runs a brief feature with an old photo from your Facebook page. You share a link to the story when it comes out, but only once, partly because you're embarrassed of that photo and partly because social media just isn't your strong suit.
- Videographer: Some members get excited by this idea and want to start on it immediately, saying you have enough money set aside for recording and can use some of that to pay for it, and that the video should be for the song on your last album that went over so great with fans. The rest of the band wants to focus on recording and worry about a video later and thinks it's stupid to make a video for an old album when you'll soon have a new one to support. Bickering ensues.
- Music supervisor: You don't have no-vox versions of your recordings. No deal.

- Studio owner: You feel weird telling him no, so you just don't contact him at all.
- Venue booker: You grab that residency starting the very next Monday and have poor draw for the first three weeks. You post it on your social media, but you don't print posters and neither does the venue. By the fourth week, your fans are starting to realize you're doing this and you get a decent turnout for the last performance, but now the residency is over and you had a weak showing overall. You ask for a Friday or Saturday and the booker says he'll call you if he needs you.

Ugh…. That sounds like hell, huh? You can avoid it by having your overall direction and your project promo strategies in place before opportunity comes knocking. You don't have to have every element perfected to start playing out, but at least know that these are tasks and decisions you will be faced with sooner than you might expect.

Event promotion:

In contrast with project promotion, event promo is designed to produce short-term, time-specific results: Butts in the seats, votes in the contest, contributions to the funding campaign, media coverage of the album release. If it has an external deadline, it's an event. It has built-in urgency.

Again, think about the difference between urgent and important. When something has urgency, it's easy to believe it is therefore inherently important. One purpose of your big-picture planning is to stay mindful of the relative importance of each event. It doesn't make sense to exhaust all of your resources (time, money, volunteers) on an event that's not that big of a deal in the grand scheme of things. Event promotion is something you will need to do repeatedly, so pace yourself.

Only you can decide how to gauge the importance of your events. Your criteria won't be the same as other artists', because your goals aren't the same. For one band, getting added to the bill of a big summer show in a resort town will be massively important because the tourist circuit is what they want most. For another band, that same booking is just a paycheck because their core audience is teens on YouTube. Either way, you should obviously give 100% during the performance—that's your integrity and reputation at stake. But the amount of work you do behind the scenes (and the amount of money you budget for paid advertising such as boosted social media posts) to capitalize on that booking will vary depending on how closely aligned it is with your overall strategy.

Now recall the difference between tasks and projects: A project is a set of tasks, and large projects usually have sub-projects, each of which is itself a set of related tasks. In those terms, then, your band is an open-ended, ongoing project and your events are sub-projects with clearly defined pre-, during-, and post-event tasks. Thinking this way helps you to remember the scope of what you're doing as you bounce between project and event promotion day-to-day.

Event promotion operates on a different timeline than project promotion. You could say it's a faster tempo. Each event might run at, say, 240 BPM, and then stop. Yet underlying all of your events and filling the spaces between them, you have your 60-BPM project promotion, steadily carrying on.

When your project promotion is well-established and running smoothly, you have context for all of the decisions to be made in event promotion. You're not choosing poster colors based on your mood that day; you're choosing them based on the colors of your branding set. You're not hanging posters wherever you can find a parking place; you're hanging them according to your street-teaming plan. You're not dropping in a social media post whenever you think of it; you're following a schedule. And the language you use in those social media posts sounds consistent because you've given thought to the online "voice" of the band and everyone who posts as the band writes in that voice.

Starting with all of these parameters in place makes event promotion fairly straightforward. Check out the Event Promotion Grid in Chapter 14 for a sample timeline and tasks.

•

So promotion is either project-focused or event-focused. Now let's look at another way to categorize it.

Terrestrial, Digital, & Relational Promotion

Promotional activities, at both the project level and the event level, fall into three basic categories: terrestrial, digital, and relational. The first two are probably familiar to you, and the third soon will be.

Terrestrial systems:

Terrestrial promotion is everything done with assets in the physical world, for example postering, merchandising, radio station mail-outs, and printed press kits. Many of the tasks of terrestrial promotion are repetitive, which means they're fairly easy to organize: You figure out your process the first time, write it down, and then follow that process the next time without having to figure it out again.

Terrestrial promotion is difficult to do as a one-person operation, because it's time-consuming and requires your physical presence, but since it's so easy to capture in a checklist or step-by-step instructions, it's also an area where volunteers can help immensely.

Digital systems:

Digital promotion is everything that's done in the virtual world, which is much more than terrestrial nowadays. It includes your website, email newsletters, EPK, music distribution and streaming platforms (iTunes, Google Play, Spotify, Pandora, YouTube, Concert Window), online calendar and directory sites where you post your EPK or list your shows (Sonicbids, Bandsintown, ReverbNation, Bandcamp, Pollstar), and all of your social media accounts.

Because digital promotion is essential, some basic ability with a computer and smartphone is also essential for every DIY musician. If you grew up with technology, this is probably just a way of life for you. If you've been in music since before computers were a thing, you might be having some discomfort with transitioning into the digital world. It probably won't ever come naturally for you; just know that it's worth the effort to learn.

Relational systems:

Relational promotion is directly person-to-person. It includes all two-way forms of communication, whether in person, on the phone, by email, on social media, or even by a letter in the mail (those still happen), so there is overlap with digital and terrestrial. The key distinction is that it involves back-and-forth interaction, or at least an attempt at it, not just one-way information delivery. This section continues the discussion of relationships that we started in Chapter 7.

Your most crucial form of relational promotion is your live performances. The event promotion ended when you took the stage, but your overall project promotion is ongoing, and it's at peak power when you're onstage. It's important to stay in that promotion mindset when you have an audience, because you have many brief promo opportunities throughout the show: When you say the band's name, invite the crowd to follow you on social media and streaming services, high-five a fan up front, mention a town or a wedding you just played, point out the merch table, or reference the upcoming album or tour ... all of your banter and interaction is relational promotion, so make it intentional.

The "performance" doesn't end with the last song. When you hop offstage, you still have another set: Fan greetings, ideally near the merch table. All of those autographs and photos contribute to building your fan community, which brings you not just show attendance and album sales but sometimes business opportunities as well.

Media appearances are another form of performance, whether it's live on TV or radio, or on the phone or in person with a print reporter. While you want to come across as genuine, you also need to take care to present yourself in a way that furthers your career goals.

Anything you do in which you're representing your music business person-to-person is a form of relational promotion. This is another thing you have in common with all self-employed people: We're aware that everything we do is a potential reflection on the business, and we're always poised for networking opportunities. (Jump back to Chapter 7 if you need a refresher on networking.)

Relational promotion is arguably the hardest type. It's time-consuming and requires your physical presence, same as terrestrial, but it's not a job you can completely delegate to others. If you have hired help (manager, agent, PR, merch support), they certainly can and should help with networking, but they can't fill in for artists during fan meet & greets or media interviews. As an entertainer, and especially if you're a solo artist or the frontperson of the band, like it or not you're the show pony and there are times when one of your pack mules just isn't enough.

●

The rest of this chapter covers the main promotional activities that you'll need or want to make use of. Depending on how you're using it, each activity fits into more than one of the above categories. Recognizing how they work for project and/or event promotion and which aspects of each activity are terrestrial, digital, or relational will help you to keep a mental grip on what you're doing and why.

Bios and EPK

Describing yourself might be one of the hardest things you have to do, but you must do it. You can't just wait for the press to paint a picture of you. First, it's unlikely you'll get any media attention, let alone bookings, if you can't describe your sound and give some basic background about yourself. Second, if by chance you get a surprise media mention, you might not like what they come up with in the absence of any insights from you. Far better to direct the message yourself.

Below are the basic elements you need. Start with whichever seems easiest and let it inform what you write for the others. In the end, all of these elements should coordinate anyway, so it doesn't matter which you do first. Don't overthink this—just write them. They don't have to be perfect or permanent, but they need to exist ASAP.

An easy way to make a system of this is to start a Word doc with each of the following elements, noting the word counts of each, so you have them all handy to copy and paste as needed. Going forward, you can update all of your bios in the same document and copy in variations that you have used for different purposes. You could also keep a running list in this same doc of every site you need to update when you make a major change to your bio.

One-phrase descriptions:

These give an indication of your genre, the mood of a song or of your music overall, or the most noticeable element of your act: "hard-driving southern rock," "dreamy synth pop," "welcoming folk vibe," "profound lyrics on a spare melodic base," "roof-shaking stage show." In your wildest fantasies, what would you hope a reviewer would say about you? Say those things about yourself.

While these descriptors are subjective, they shouldn't be so artsy that they really don't say anything: "A Minnesotan's fever dream" or "the love child of Yoko Ono and Willie Nelson" sounds clever but doesn't effectively preview your music or your act. Dig deeper and come up with actual descriptions.

Short bio:

Describe your act in 50-100 words. Include your stage name or the full name of the band, the acronym if you use one, and the information you most want to highlight (what makes you different, what makes you the best, etc.). Include your website, which will be the jumping-off point for all of your other online accounts.

You'll use this short bio often: In the short description field of all of your social media, music streaming, and promotion platform profiles; when applying for festivals, contests, and other opportunities; when requested by venues to promote your show through their channels or by media ahead of live appearances, and more. You don't want to have to write a new one every time, so create a basic one now that you can use as-is or lightly edit to fit a specific situation.

Long bio:

This is your full story to date. It doesn't have to include absolutely everything and definitely shouldn't be an extended ramble, but it should have the level of detail that a superfan would be interested to read. The most straightforward approach is a basic chronological history of how your act came to be, but you can structure it like a *Rolling Stone* interview/feature, a Wikipedia entry, a first-person journal entry, or whatever is most natural for you.

This bio will always be a work in progress. As you release new music, get new media coverage, gather more wins, and perhaps overcome notable obstacles, you'll add them to this bio. Over time you might also delete some lesser points to keep the focus on what's most important.

Speaking of Wikipedia, you will be eligible to have a Wikipedia entry when you've reached a certain level of credibility or attention that can be substantiated by independent sources. You can't just write a Wikipedia entry about yourself—it's supposed to be written about you by someone else, and it has to cite published sources other than you. When you get to this level, you can allow your Wikipedia entry to be the full history of the band and not worry about forcing your long bio to do that job.

Electronic press kit (EPK):

There are exceptions, but the electronic press kit or EPK is now almost universally preferred over a printed kit in a folder—so much so that the term "EPK" has replaced "press kit" in general parlance. In addition to being digital vs. physical, your EPK should be made available or delivered as a web link, not an email attachment.

There are many ways to create an EPK, so don't get hung up on searching for the single right way to do this. You can create it from scratch using Microsoft Word or Google Docs (like a resume), or use an EPK builder like the one included with Sonicbids accounts, which also gives you the option of formatting the info for printing if needed. What's important is that you choose a format you can realistically maintain and then keep it up to date.

Your EPK should contain:

- Music links (set to public and streamable but not necessarily downloadable)
- Video links (set to public; can be on any platform or directly on your website)
- Long and short bios
- High-resolution publicity photo (posed; you can also include an excellent live shot if you have one)
- Names and roles/instruments of all members
- Contact info (at least a general email, but also management or booking contacts if different)
- Social media links
- Discography (list of published music with titles and dates)
- High-res album cover art
- Upcoming shows link
- Data on your typical draw if known (don't lie)
- Good press quotes if you have them with links to the full articles

A variation on the EPK is a "one-sheet," which is useful to include when mailing a press release, physical CD, or flash drive to a reporter, radio station, or talent buyer. Your one-sheet contains the highlights of your EPK (best photo, short bio, discography, latest news, key statistics, contact info), and should also include the full URLs of your complete EPK, website, and social media accounts. You can set these URLs as hyperlinks in a PDF version, but you also need the full addresses in the printed version, so don't use the convention of a hyperlinked "click here" in the text of a one-sheet.

Photos and Videos

These assets are second only to your music in their importance to your branding. Unlike your music, though, you have only partial control of how you are portrayed through photos and videos. A clear branding strategy will direct your decisions about these assets when they are within your power to make, and it will also help you to exert some influence over which fan images become most closely associated with your act.

Publicity photos and videos:

It's standard practice to have at least one posed photo for publicity purposes. This is a multipurpose image that you can use on posters and online show listings, send to reporters and bloggers to accompany features about you or reviews of your music, and advance to venues to help promote your shows through their channels.

Publicity photos don't have to cost a ton of money. The most important considerations are that they portray you the way you want to be portrayed and that they are a high enough resolution ("high-res") to look good both online and when printed. If you have no budget for a studio session complete with lighting and wardrobe, but you have a photographer friend with a good-quality camera, you can get a perfectly respectable starter photo without all the fanfare. In fact, your photographer friend will have an easier time capturing authentic expressions because you'll be more at ease with him or her than with a hired stranger.

These photos will need to be updated from time to time. Plan on (and budget for) a fresh photo shoot with every big benchmark (album release, major tour) or every couple of years, with increasingly high quality as your career progresses. During these group photo sessions, also get individual shots of the lead singer and each of the core bandmembers; you can use these to create bio sections about each member on your website and social media, and they'll also serve you if you do some small acoustic shows without the full band.

A publicity video is not necessary at the very beginning of your career, but it will become increasingly important as you go for more competitive bookings such as festivals and out-of-town venues where the decision-makers wouldn't have the chance to prescreen you live, even on the off-chance that they would have the time or interest to do so. When you reach that point, you won't want to rely on fans' YouTube videos for this purpose. So, after you have some live performance experience and you're ready to reach for the next level, consider hiring a professional videographer to shoot one of your shows and edit the footage down to a two- to four-minute highlight video (sometimes referred to as a "sizzle reel"). Decide in advance whether you will record the live audio from the same show, and if so from the sound board or from the room with good condenser mics, or whether you will have the videographer sync audio from your studio recordings with the video footage. The costs of each of these options varies, so discuss it all in advance with each of the hired professionals involved in the project.

Also at this point, consider the stability of the band. You want this video to last you at least a year, so if personnel changes are in the works, it's probably not the best time to create something meant to represent you into the future. On the other hand, if bandmembers tend to come and go in your world, don't put off creating this key promo asset: Instruct the videographer to focus more on the core members (i.e. you and whoever you believe is with you for the long haul), avoid lengthy shots of side players who aren't part of the band's visual identity, and choose the final cuts with an eye toward whether the video will still work months from now if some of the players depicted are no longer part of the live show.

Your promo videos can be posted to your YouTube channel, from which you can generate a link to embed a viewer on your website, and your videos can also be uploaded directly to Facebook. As of this writing, posting "native" to Facebook in this way will get you more organic (i.e. unpaid) views than sharing a YouTube link.

Fan pix & vids:

Some artists cringe at the very thought of fan cellphone photos, or worse, videos. Y'all—this is happening, whether you want it to or not. You can either keep hating it, ignore the posts, and let Google and YouTube decide which assets are going to come up first in searches on your band … or you can embrace this phenomenon and apply some creative control.

Encourage fans to post their photos from the show and tag you in them. My band clients have had great luck with fan photos on Instagram. Reshare with the person's handle so they get credit (Repost is a great app for this), and save the photo to use again later (with the photographer's handle embedded in the corner) on Facebook and Twitter.

Look for photos that are in focus, with interesting composition (either as they are, or if you crop to a key area) and non-weird facial expressions. If the resolution could use a little boost, apply the Sharpen function. In many cases, that's all you'll have to do to make it a spectacular photo.

With videos, accept the reality that the audio will probably be mediocre, the video will usually be dark, and fans will choose to post your covers more often than your originals. It's all maddening, I know, but again, you can't beat 'em so you'll be wise to join 'em. If your performance was decent and the clip looks and sounds okay by cellphone standards, reshare and tag. The assets you give attention to will be most likely to get more engagement overall and will then migrate to the top of web searches on your band's name.

Why and how to namecheck fans:

I'm big on giving credit. First because it's not cool to use people's intellectual property without crediting them, and even a simple cellphone pic counts as intellectual property.

Second, I encourage it because thanking fans by name builds community. Many fans hesitate to post their photos, videos, or even statuses tagging the band because they're not sure the band would want or like it, so you need to let them know you welcome it!

Whenever you invite fans to share and tag their images of you, mention that you'll tag them back when you reshare. That promise of tagging them in the reshare will be encouraging to most fans, and—bonus—it will also discourage the rare occasional person who doesn't want you "using" their stuff.

Remind them that on Facebook, the post has to be public for you to be able to see it, even if they tagged your page. Also note that a Facebook page can't technically tag a person, so be sure to name them in the caption and include their Insta or Twitter handle if they gave one: "Thanks to Megan Bandfan (@megzluvsmusic) for this awesome photo!"

This quote or something similar rewritten in your own style would be a great addition to every social media event you create: "We LOVE fan photos! Feel free to grab a cellphone pic at our shows and post & tag us! We'll reshare our favorites and tag you back!"

Serious/professional photographers:

There are two ways you'll encounter professional or skilled amateur photographers and videographers: You'll make arrangements with them before they shoot, or they'll simply shoot your show and you might see the results after.

Some venues have a "house photographer"—a professional who shoots some or all of the performances staged in that space. You might or might not be told in advance that the venue has a house photographer, and your access to those photos will vary from club to club. If you receive detailed advance info from the venue or producer, this is one of the items that might be included (one of many reasons to read the entire advance). Professional live music photographer Annette Crawford advises, "Ask the club you're playing at if they have a house photographer, and if so, what their arrangement is. I'm the house photographer at a club in San Antonio, and any photos I take are posted to their Flickr page. The artists are free to use them, as long as they use my watermark."

Whenever you see photos with a watermark—the photographer's name or company imprinted on the photo—that's a sign that this person is either a serious hobbyist or a professional. Never crop out a watermark! If you like the photo and want to reshare it, leave that credit right where they put it and also be sure to tag them. If they have a Facebook page, tag it as an extra courtesy.

Photojournalists:

Festivals and other large productions will usually allow photographers from media outlets to shoot each set, with some limitations. Check your advance for answers to these questions, or if these details are of particular concern to you, ask before you hit the stage:

- Will there be a photo pit (a fenced area directly in front of the stage that is reserved for credentialed photographers)?
- Will photographers/videographers be allowed to come onstage?
- Will flash be allowed?
- Will they be allowed to shoot only the first three songs (the usual limit) or the entire performance?

You'll also want to know what your options will be for use of the photos and videos after the show. You might be given the option to purchase images you like, or you might get to share them on social media only after they're published, same as every other viewer.

Paying for unsolicited images:

It's such a blessing to have an excellent photographer unexpectedly grace your show. You get fantastic free assets and it's an easy way to find photographers you would like to hire down the road. However, don't be pressured into paying for images that you didn't ask for in the first place. You might occasionally receive an email from someone who shot one of your shows and is now offering to sell you the photos. If there's an image in there that you absolutely adore and the price is reasonable (no more than, say, $50 for a high-resolution image and the right to use it however you want), it's probably a good deal. But know this: You are never obligated to pay for a service you didn't request.

Your band photographers:

If you intend to bring your own photographer/videographer to a show, plan ahead to ensure that person gets the access s/he needs. Find out what credentials will be required (crew laminate or wristband, press pass, guest list, comp ticket, etc.) and what rules or limitations the person will have to follow, then advance that info to the photographer before the day of the show.

Be mindful of your photographers' behavior at your shows. Everyone connected to your act is a reflection on you, so make sure they are aware of necessary courtesies such as sharing space with other photographers, not getting in the sound engineers' way, not moving monitors or adjusting lighting, and avoiding excessive blocking of fans' sightlines to the stage.

Clarify in advance whether you expect or will allow them to come onstage, and if so, how far. No performer wants to be surprised by a camera inches from their face. Also, attendees aren't especially thrilled with looking at photographers' backs onstage in front of the band, so consider keeping them offstage unless you're shooting an official video, in which case be sure to tell the audience so they can project maximum exuberance.

Live-streaming

The fan experience of live-streaming falls somewhere between video after the event and the sensory richness of in-person attendance. As of this writing, it's the newest form of promotion/social media posting/asset creation/fan engagement. In other words, it's a weird and wonderful hybrid of many functions.

Broadcasting live can be as simple as an impromptu cellphone capture, or it can be a carefully planned and produced online performance using actual cameras and an audio feed from the sound board. You can originate a stream from a growing number of apps and platforms, both within and beyond social media and ranging from casual to high-end professional. Options include Periscope, Facebook Live, YouTube Live, Google Hangouts, and Concert Window. Each way has its place, but be sure to make an informed choice about it rather than throwing up a half-baked stream just to have something to show.

Keep in mind that, unless the venue or producer has initiated live-streaming of your show or is getting a cut of any revenue from the stream, they're doing you a favor by allowing you to broadcast. Some venues dislike it because they are concerned it will reduce in-person attendance; some sound engineers resent it because bands make it their problem when glitches arise. It's up to you whether to ask permission beforehand or forgiveness after, but as with any process, you'll have less potential for failure if you're upfront about it and give everyone involved the chance to prepare.

Allow time to set up and test your streaming equipment as part of soundcheck, but again, unless streaming is part of your performance agreement, don't inconvenience venue staff or other bands by delaying their normal process for something that is not a key element of the live show. If it's as simple as pointing your cellphone at the lead vocal mic, that's not a big intrusion. But if you have cameras on tripods or if you need to draw audio from the board, the safest route is to include that information in the stage plot and inputs list that you advance to the venue. If you spring it on the sound engineer when you get there, you risk overwhelming or irritating him or her and compromising the overall sound quality, both in person and online.

If you promised to live-stream a show, for example through teasers on social media, don't wait until load-in to figure out how you're going to do it. That advice goes double if you presold tickets for the stream on a platform like Concert Window. If you're just getting into streaming and you want fans to know you're going to try it, but you're worried it won't work, it's fine to say that in the promo. Aim for that ideal balance of professionalism (diligent preparation) and authenticity (showing you're human)—something like:

"Hey guys, we're trying something new with the next show! For you out-of-towners, we'll be live-streaming on [platform], so be sure to tune in. Apologies in advance if we have any technical glitches—we'll do our best to make it work!"

Online Presence

This is the collection of sites and apps where you exist in the digital world. It is massive, convoluted, and labyrinthine, and it poses a high risk of becoming a productivity black hole for you and your helpers. It is also utterly essential to your success, so it's worth investing time up front to plan your approach to all of the following elements.

Website:

This is your online home base. Before the rise of social media, it was the only place other than live shows that fans could have an interactive experience with you, so it was imperative to keep your website dynamic, interesting, and different with each visit.

Nowadays, because of social media, websites can rest a bit easier. You will no longer be dismissed by fans and reporters for having a static, brochure-like website if you also have an active social media presence. So think of your website in the same way that you think of your physical home: It's a place to store all of your stuff, even if you don't spend much time there.

Here are the most common sections or components of a band website. You can have more than this if you like (but do take care not to make the site overly cluttered):

- No-hassle links to play your music. Choose a plug-in or widget that performs this function as simply as possible. Each link should also have a clear path for purchasing the song, jumping to the album, and/or jumping back to your full catalog.
- A prominent link to your show calendar. Imagine the tipsy fan out with her friends, tapping on her phone in a strobe-lit bar, trying to look up your show as everyone's deciding where to go next. Your website needs to make it easy for her.
- Great photos. Choose your best posed and live shots for showcasing on your website. Make them downloadable for bookers and reporters to grab on the fly. If you also have great videos, include those links or embed the videos directly into your site.
- A bio that is brief enough to be read in one sitting but long enough to provide key info and generate further interest in your music, live show, or full life story. Include a link to your EPK here and also in your Contact Us section.
- Links to your social media accounts. You can also include widgets that show the most recent post or posts on each platform.

- A link or field to sign up for your email list, if you have one.
- Clear contact instructions for talent buyers, reporters, and fans. This can be just email; if you're using outside PR or booking, those reps should also have a phone number you can list, but if you're handling it all yourself, you're not expected or advised to post your personal phone number. Include another link to your EPK here, near the booking contact instructions.

If you choose to manage your own website, keep a list of all the templates, plug-ins, and widgets you have, including the name, login and PW if any, date you last updated it, recurring cost if any, and renewal date. You must keep these all up to date for security purposes, even if it seems like your site is running just fine, so having them listed in one place will make it easier to remember what you have and to do a quick check when new attacks come out. Watch for articles and blog posts like Wordfence's "Top 50 Most Attacked WordPress Plugins This Week" and update or change any of yours that are vulnerable.

Social media accounts:

If you haven't already, create social media accounts for your band or act that are separate from your personal accounts. This is similar to keeping your personal and business bank accounts separate. Depending on the platform, you might still have some overlap of business contacts in your personal accounts, but you definitely want business accounts for promotion and fan interaction. As of this writing, the basics are a Facebook page and a band Twitter and Instagram account. The jury is out on Snapchat; some bands and fans enjoy it, but there's no clear indication that it's creating connections in ways that the other platforms can't.

A YouTube channel is also a basic item. Functionally it's a hybrid of social media and website; how, and how heavily, you use it will depend on how integral videos are to your business and how frequently you produce new ones.

We all know social media can be a bottomless pit of lost time. So the first imperative here is to respect that it's a dangerous tool and use it carefully, intentionally, and only while sober. ;) To keep your social media from devolving into a chaotic, neglected mess, decide your posting frequency and stick with it. Do not overcommit! It is far better to post once a week, every week, than to post five things in one day, nothing for the next five weeks, and then another bunch of posts all at once.

At a minimum, social media needs to be a part of promotion for each of your performances and other events. This applies whether you're posting as the band or as a musician playing with one or more bands. When you build social media in as a promo step for every show, you'll end up creating a consistent posting presence without having to follow a social media calendar per se.

To go beyond the basic show-promo track, you can post about your life behind the scenes (I use the hashtags #bandlife, #musicianlife, and #indiemusician for these); share articles and other posts about music and other topics of interest to you within your branding scope; or invite fans to chat with you on random topics like their current favorite Netflix show.

The "band life" track is always of interest to fans because it gives them a glimpse backstage while also humanizing you and giving them reasons to like you as a person, not just a performer. Use photos and short videos to show them the things that amuse or delight you: The endless array of band posters on the walls at a cool old club, the sheer size of the stage at your first festival gig, the look on your dog's face when you come home from a tour. Even a quick snapshot of the inside of your rehearsal space or of the sun setting behind the venue as you wait for your stage call makes an easy post that will likely get good engagement. Remember, what seems like a boring moment to you will often be fascinating to your fans.

The "topics" track gives you a platform for talking about and supporting other interests that are important to you (for example, Michael Franti posts frequently about his Do It For The Love nonprofit wish-granting foundation). These topics don't have to be related to your music career, but they should be carefully chosen to align with your branding message. Consider whether your opinions might turn fans off, and if so, whether you're willing to take that stand: Some bands do, and those positions become part of their brand identity.

The "fan chat" track gives fans direct opportunities to interact with you, again letting them see you as human and potentially converting them from casual fans to superfans. These are fun filler posts that don't require an accompanying photo or link. You might not get a lot of response to them at first, when your number of followers is relatively low; there's nothing wrong with private-messaging your friends and asking them to comment on these posts to get things moving.

You can use this multi-track system on just one of your platforms (whichever gets the most engagement), or on all of them if it makes sense in your time budget. Check out the sample Social Media Calendar in Chapter 14 for one way to organize and schedule your social media posts by platform and track.

Promotion platforms:

While social media is where you converse with fans, promotion platforms such as Bandcamp, ReverbNation, Bandsintown, Soundcloud, and Sonicbids can be used to simply inform them (and talent buyers and the media). Now, each of these platforms would much prefer that you use them for interaction as well, but you have to make careful choices about how you use your limited time. A more realistic approach is to direct fans to your social media sites to ask questions and keep up with your day-to-day happenings.

As with social media, consider the time investment required to maintain each of these platforms. It does make sense to have a presence on each one (and there are dozens), but it doesn't have to be an active presence: You can choose which platform is the most valuable and create a dynamic, full-content profile there, then post just the basics (band name, photo, website, socials, tour dates) on all of the others.

To choose your primary platform, look at what each offers and determine which functions are most important to you. Is it the easy EPK builder on Sonicbids? Is it the music discovery community on Bandcamp? Whichever one has the most of what you want is the logical choice to be your primary focus.

Unlike social media, it is smart to standardize the look and contents of each of your promotion platform profiles. Using the same photos, bio, and links on each one makes upkeep efficient and reinforces your branding. This will make them redundant, which you avoid on your social media accounts, but here it's fine because you want fans to know that they're seeing info on the same band from one site to the next.

Why not choose just one promotion platform and bypass the rest? Here are two good reasons: You don't want another band with the same name to take "your" place on a site and confuse your branding, and you do want your show listings posted in as many places as you can possibly manage. This will often mean manually posting dates on five or more sites, which is time-consuming and boring, but it will pay off in greater search engine visibility, more show notifications to fans not only through your socials but through the apps of the platforms they subscribe to, and therefore, theoretically, in better draw and bigger bookings down the road.

A final note on promotion platforms: Some of them have not just the fan-facing element which is your (usually) free band profile but also a behind-the-scenes, subscribers-only business section that you can use to apply for gigs and licensing opportunities. Some opportunities are listed on all of the major sites, but some partner with one site exclusively.

For example, Sonicbids is the only application site for South By Southwest, and ReverbNation is the sole application site for Summerfest. If this functionality matters to you, determine which site will give you the most value for your subscription fee, invest in it, and use it fully. Note that the one you choose as your primary promotion platform might not be the same one you choose for paid access to opportunities; this is fine as long as you can keep up with the admin tasks of each.

Merchandising

Branded merchandise is a revenue stream (sometimes a big one!) and it's also a key promotional tool. But it has its challenges too. In addition to costing you money upfront and adding to the load at load-in, it can limit your schmoozing time after the show or cost you extra if you hire someone to run it.

This is another situation where engaging your fans' assistance can be a huge help. The Roosevelts (WeAreTheRoosevelts.com) have had good success with this. Frontman James Mason says they keep a database of fans in each city who have expressed interest in helping out in this way in exchange for free tickets to the show. Before each tour, they contact those fans to arrange merch coverage, ensuring that the person can arrive early to get oriented to details including prices and the credit card system, and be ready to sell when doors open. "It's a huge savings to have fans run merch for you, and it's also a huge boost," James notes. "We get to spend more time interacting after the show vs. being stuck behind the table doing the sales. It's a game changer for sure." Whenever possible, says James, they would rather guest-list a fan than hire a stranger to do it because "it's way better to have your fans selling something they actually believe in."

You'll have to extend some trust regarding the money, but a fan is unlikely to steal from you. Most of your transactions will probably be card sales anyway. More important is coaching your volunteers on how to keep an eye on the cash, the products, and the equipment so nothing walks away.

The downside to having one of your best fans running merch is that s/he won't get to enjoy the show up-close. One solution is to have two friends share the job—one stays at the table while the other gets some show time, then they trade. Let them watch from sidestage so they can get up close mid-show. If you have a high volume of sales, you'll do well to have two people working before and after the show anyway, so it will be worth the extra guest-list spot.

Another option, which The Roosevelts prefer, is to close the merch table during the show. The volunteer handles pre-show sales, then throws a black cloth over the table, stashes the money and iPads, enjoys the performance, then hurries back at the end for the after-show buying frenzy. Along with your "thank you, good night!" be sure to announce from the stage that you'll be at the merch table for meet & greet, and then hustle over there as fast as you can. There's a Merch Kit Checklist and a sample set of Merch Procedures in Chapter 14.

As you grow, you'll get booked into bigger venues and festivals where merch sales will be handled for you. It's a mixed blessing in that you don't have to recruit fans to handle it, but you do have to pay a flat fee, or a percentage of sales, or both. Either way, that habit of dashing to the merch area after the show will continue to pay off in more sales and stronger fan retention.

Media Coverage

Getting people to buy your music and come to your shows is greatly assisted when the media amplifies your message. A positive album review or show preview is the media equivalent of a networking introduction from a VIP contact. Show reviews and feature articles are like having a master networker talking you up to all of his or her contacts. This makes ongoing media outreach worthy of priority placement in your promo plan and schedule.

One mistake that veteran music journalist Kevin Curtin sees time and time again is bands asking for a write-up simply because they exist. What works, he says, is including details about why you're interesting and why you should have a story right now.

"There's never an article just like, 'Cool band alert! This is a cool band! And here's a picture of four white guys leaning up against a brick wall and they're all dressed cool,'" says Kevin. "That doesn't tell you anything about the band. Every song, every album, every band has a hundred different cool stories behind it, so, without telling reporters exactly what to write, give them some piece of information that piques their interest and makes them think about how they could turn that into an interesting story."

Contacting the media has a lot in common with contacting bookers and with networking in general. Courtesy and concision will help you to stand out, and a strategy for timely contact, reasonable follow-up, and ongoing touches will put you in front of the right eyes at the right time. Still, it's all cold-calling until you have developed those contacts. This is why so many artists turn to paid promotion when they can afford it.

Hiring a PR rep or publicist:

As with every other aspect of the biz, there is hired help available to support your promotional efforts. You can utilize a publicist, or more broadly a public relations representative or firm, for both project and event promotion. Ongoing PR tends to focus more on the project, with activations for key events but also publicity not connected to a specific event such as feature articles and radio play. It's designed to keep the artist consistently in the public eye, even when there's nothing fresh to promote. A publicist in the purest sense of the title has a narrower scope than a PR rep, focusing solely on obtaining media coverage for events (shows, tours, music releases, etc.). Keep in mind that the duties and scope of these roles are not universally agreed upon, so don't assume based on a person's title that you know exactly what s/he will do for you.

If you're disorganized, hiring PR or even a single-event publicist is not the solution. In fact, you need to be fairly organized already before these professionals will be able to help you. "More and more, artists are having to 'do it yourself' in order to get noticed not only by the industry, but even with publicists and other potential team members," says Heather Wagner Reed, president and founder of Austin-based PR firm Juice Consulting. "When an artist comes to me with a sharp-looking website, great PR photos, and some serious action on social media, not only am I impressed, but I am also more likely to dive in quickly."

Here are some things you need to do to get maximum benefit from a hired PR/publicity engagement:

- Understand that you have to pay for this. As we talked about in Chapter 1, this is a form of purchasing more time, and it's also a form of renting influence. If you're not ready for this level of expenditure, continue using the resources that have gotten you this far and build up to hiring PR down the road.
- Understand that you must be worthy of representation. Professional reps extend their relationship equity on your behalf, ideally opening doors that would have otherwise remained closed to you. Therefore you need to have something worth promoting. Reps who are both ethical and experienced will decline to work with you if they believe your act isn't ready for greater attention or for the demands on your time and talent that will come with that attention. However, there are unethical people who will gladly take your money even if you're not yet ready, so do a ruthlessly honest evaluation of your assets and abilities before you waste money and set yourself up for failure.

- Give them enough lead time. If your album comes out in a month, you've already severely limited what a rep can do for you, no matter how great s/he is. If you think you might use professional PR down the road, even if you're just exploring the option, start reaching out at least six months ahead of the event you want supported.
- Make sure you know exactly what you are hiring: What type of outreach, which categories of markets, how many contacts, how much follow-up, etc. If the contract doesn't include radio airplay promotion, don't assume you're getting it simply because it's obvious to you that an album release should include radio outreach.
- Have your key assets ready to go. At minimum, your rep will need high-resolution publicity photos, a well-written bio and EPK, music files to share as either .MP3s or links, and accurate contact information connected to someone who will respond promptly.
- Have a clear, reliable communication plan. Identify one person to take the lead in working with the rep, make absolutely sure that person will respond quickly (minutes or hours, not days) to questions or opportunities sent by the rep, and empower that person to make decisions on the band's behalf. Review the merits of designating a band communicator in Chapter 8. Worst-case scenario: Your rep secures a media appearance for the band and does not receive confirmation from you in time, so the opportunity is lost. Put protections in place to ensure that failures like this never happen.
- Expect some form of regular activity and results report, but do not expect the rep to give you his or her contacts list. You should be able to assess what has been done on your behalf, including which outlets have been contacted and for what purpose, but you will not be given the names of the individuals your rep has reached out to. The best PR reps are effective because they have exclusive access to, and ongoing relationships with, desirable contacts.
- Give them enough time to produce results. Any publicity effort takes time to bear fruit. The nature of a publicist's or PR rep's work is relational, so they need time to introduce you to their contacts, generate interest, and provoke action (an article or blog post, music or show review, interview or appearance, etc.). For this reason, professionals in these roles will often request or even require a minimum three-month engagement.

Bottom line: You need to have your act together before you reach out to a PR professional. When you're on point, they can be too, and sometimes even faster than usual. Here's a success story from Heather Wagner Reed: "A client once came to me ready with everything from a killer bio and beautiful publicity shots, to an amazing video and website. Not to mention, a very strong single. Her EP release was just a few short weeks away, and normally I would shy away from (or even say no to) a tight deadline like that, but because she was very organized, we were literally able to activate her PR campaign in a few days and within one month she was known all over town. Till this day I tell her story to other artists because it can save you thousands of dollars in retainer fees and a ton of time to be prepared when you finally find the right PR person for your project."

•

So promotion, like booking, is a huge organizational challenge and time expense. One thing that makes it even harder than booking, though, is its unquantifiable nature: With booking, you know how you're doing based on how many gigs you're playing. It's a pass/fail. With promotion, there is no single measurable factor to tell you whether you're doing enough and/or doing it right: Attendance is impacted by your promotional efforts, but it's also impacted by the weather; the day, time, and time of year; the cover and drink prices; and by what else is happening in town at the same time. Music sales are impacted by your promotion, but in that realm you're competing for consumer dollars against multi-billion-dollar corporations including record labels, not to mention your fans' realities like rent and food.

Experience over the years and analyzing the factors you can measure will eventually help you to find a balance you can afford in both money and time. For now, your best promo tool and your only hope of not wasting time and effort is organization.

Thoughts to Ponder on Promotion

Posters don't have to be a hassle:

Services like Bandposters (www.getbandposters.com) make it easy and affordable to have posters printed and shipped to the venue. That's especially helpful when you're sending ahead for out-of-town gigs.

Use the free tools you're given:

Your social media platforms each have some level of free analytics that you can use to assess how impactful your posts are. There are also inexpensive apps that give you further analysis. Use this intel to inform your decisions about when and what to post, how to choose the demographics to target in paid ads, and even where to tour.

Avoid conflicting promotions:

If you're a busy act, you'll eventually run into this problem: You're emphasizing promotion of your next show, which is one week away, and you start getting tagged on promotion for a show that's four weeks away. Sometimes it's the venue or promoter doing it; sometimes it's another band on the bill. Either way, it can draw your fans' attention away from what you want them to be looking at right now. It's like someone changing the channel on your broadcast. You can try to prevent this by telling bookers in advance what your promotion timeline will be so they know they'll get their turn, and you can ask other bands to name but not tag you until closer to the show date. They should understand if you explain that you have other shows to promote in the meantime.

Do you need a social media management app?

Tools like Hootsuite, Buffer, Tweetdeck, and SproutSocial promise to save you hours by pulling all (in reality, it's only some) of your accounts into one screen and allowing easy cross-posting. It sounds more organized, but I don't consider them much of a value-add for a person managing their own company's social media; in fact, I have found them to be more hassle than help even for managing multiple accounts for multiple clients. Test out the free trial if you're curious.

Should you promote wallpaper gigs?

Sometimes it's hard to tell. In general, if the venue has a live music calendar and lists its upcoming acts, you're welcome to promote your show and encourage your fans to attend. However, if the venue mentions live music but doesn't name the performers, they might prefer that you blend into the background and entertain their patrons without trying to bring your own crowd. When in doubt, ask. And if you have any inkling that a gig might be private, double-check before promoting it to the public.

Eyes everywhere:

Be aware that talent buyers, promoters, reporters, and other artists are watching you on social media. They will rarely interact with your band accounts, other than to co-promote a show, but they gather much intel from your social media behavior and content.

Is radio achievable?

The consensus is that trying to get your music played on most terrestrial radio stations is pretty much futile for DIY musicians. You might have some success with independently owned local and college stations, both locally and ahead of tour stops, so consider whether those efforts fit into your promotional priorities. If you do go for it, track your spin outreach efforts and results as you do your media and booking outreach.

Counterpoint on paid PR:

If you can't afford to hire a PR professional, take heart. Relentlessly sought-after music reporter Kevin Curtin says using a publicist isn't the only way to get through to him: "For me, that just means that they have a couple thousand dollars, which is cool for them that they can pay somebody to do it for them, but if a band appeals to you with an interesting story, of course you're going to go with that no matter what source it came from."

CHAPTER 12:

ARTISTIC GROWTH

I made this the last chapter of this section because it's never-ending. Everything in the previous chapters is either startup decisions or skills that you'll build relatively quickly and then mostly coast on, with small refinements but few or no huge leaps, for the rest of your career. That's the basic, foundational business stuff. You only have to develop these procedures so far for them to serve you forever.

Do you see the irony here? In this book we're giving tons of attention to techniques for getting and keeping you organized, but it will be just fine if that peaks in a year and holds steady from there. In contrast, if you keep working at it, your musical ability will never peak. You'll continually learn new things and become steadily more proficient. Twenty years from now, you'll be using the same old tried and true organizational methods, but your musical ability will be unfathomably greater than it is today.

In other words, organization is an important thing for you to focus on in the short term, but once you have it set, all it needs is maintenance. The far more important thing for the entire span of your career is your ongoing development as a musician.

So how will you prioritize that? In what ways will you build artistic growth into your daily routine? This just might be the most important-but-not-urgent element of your life. How will you fulfill it?

Organizing Your Practice

Whether or not it's formally named, "continuing education" is a necessity in every field. Licensed professions (medicine, counseling, law, teaching, etc.) require it to ensure that practitioners remain competent to do their work. In music, you're not legally or even ethically required to continue learning and to keep your skills sharp—you just won't go as far if you don't. Making time for gigs is easy compared to making time for practice. Remember externally controlled vs. self-controlled time from Chapter 1? Gigs are externally controlled time: You made a commitment to do them. Practice is self-controlled time: The commitment is only to yourself, which makes it easier to break, unless you have a system for protecting that commitment.

Protect your practice time:

Perhaps you naturally gravitate toward practicing every day and you don't need to formally schedule it. Music is a self-soothing necessity for so many musicians ... it might be that nothing can pull you away from it for more than a day or two. Then again, life intrudes and you might find yourself sacrificing your music time for other responsibilities. Not only will this deplete your spirit, it will also reduce your skill. Remember the "Big Rocks First" lesson from Chapter 1: Block out time daily or at whatever regular frequency is best for you—not just what you think you have time for, but what you truly want. Then don't let your practice get crowded out by anything other than a rare, true emergency.

Make it productive:

One thing that makes it tempting to skip your individual practice is not having anything specific that you want to do with the time. If you're tired of your warmups and you know the songs you need to know for now, you might feel like you don't need to practice this time.

You can plan ahead to avoid this boredom reaction. Structure your practices with as much or as little complexity as you like, but include a few basic elements:

- Skill maintenance. Do some of your well-worn exercises every time, both to warm up and to reinforce the neural pathways and muscle memory that keep these skills sharp. Or if you're bored with your usual stuff, take this time to look up or invent some new ones.
- Practice the songs you're currently responsible for performing. If running through them quickly works for you, i.e. if you don't need to practice at the same quality that you perform, do that. There is research about whether practicing at less than 100% is helpful or harmful—go online and read those debates if you're curious.
- Play with old stuff. Run through songs that used to be on your setlist or favorites that you're still nostalgic about.
- Play with new stuff. Try out songs you've heard and liked lately or noodle around with new ideas of your own.
- Keep track of your progress. Use a notebook or app to document where you are by date as you go along. Similar to tracking your weight or measurements when you're trying to change your body composition, keep track of your musical skill development with key measurements to benchmark your progress. If you're trying to expand your vocal range, keep track of when you master the next note and the next. If you've challenged yourself to write songs at a certain pace, document your progress on that. Finishing each practice session with some progress notes and measurements sets you up for another intention-driven session tomorrow.

If you do a bit of each of these in each practice, you will have touched on past, present, and future, and given yourself some latitude to introduce variety while still attending to your fundamentals. If the reality is that you often get interrupted and have to cut your practice sessions short, structure your time in priority order. The order of the five points above might be a good way to go: If you get through at least the first two, you will have covered the fundamentals. Catch up your progress tracking the next chance you get, and squeeze in the fun stuff as often as possible.

Below are more things I see musicians doing to keep their artistic growth from being drowned out by the relentlessness of life.

Thoughts to Ponder on Artistic Growth

Seek out new situations:

Look for ways to get exposed to new ideas and meet new people. Are there any songwriters' meetups or song circles in your area? Where are the open mics? Is anyone doing song-swap performances?

Learn more instruments:

If you're a singer, it would be natural for you to learn piano. If you play lead guitar, learn bass and vice versa. You don't have to develop your playing of these instruments to the point that you could perform them live ... you can learn just enough to use them while composing, to better understand the progress and roadblocks your bandmates are experiencing, and to enrich your relationship with your primary instrument.

Teach someone about music:

Even if you don't teach formal lessons, take advantage of chances to show someone a little bit of what you do. If a social media follower says he really liked a particular verse, share a bit about what inspired it. If a fan admires your guitar after the show, tell her something about how it plays ("Yeah, I really like how this one stays in tune") or explain what you're doing as you change a string. When people hear you're a musician and say, "Oh yeah, I play [whatever] too," don't get into a competition about who's better or more experienced; instead, ask something like, "What's your favorite part about it?" The best way to keep learning something is to teach it, even in little moments like these.

Learn to play from and create charts:

A song chart, or chord chart, is a specialized form of note-taking to document how the song is played. You don't have to be able to read music to create or use charts. In organizational terms, song charts are like checklists to remind you of the steps of a job. They make your individual practice more efficient and more accurate, and they enable substitute or side players in rotation to step in on a moment's notice. The ability to show up and play a piece of music having never rehearsed it is a major career advantage, and having all of your music charted is a safety net that can make the difference between canceling a gig vs. going on with subs. Apps such as OnSong make digital charting easy.

Watch other bands:

When time allows, check out the other acts on the bill with you or go out to other bands' shows, not just for networking but also for your own self-assessment. Learn from them whether they're above or below your skill level. Which elements of theirs need development? Which are they excelling at? This isn't about whether you like their music and it's not about being that smug jerk who thinks everyone else sucks. It's about giving yourself perspective for measuring your own progress.

Think of your body as part of your instrument:

If you're a vocalist, your body literally is your instrument, but there is a level of physicality to every other instrument as well, and also to entertaining in general. Look around at veteran musicians, but instead of focusing on the ones for whom hard living has taken its toll, seek out indie artists who have made physical self-care a priority. California-based vocalist Earl Thomas is a remarkable example of an internationally touring performer whose attention to nutrition and exercise has been a key factor in his 30-plus years as an independent artist.

Read:

Read books and blogs, fiction or nonfiction, that expand your emotional intelligence, world view, and vocabulary. This is valuable for every artist but especially so for lyricists. In the literary genre of music, biographies of artists are good but autobiographies are even better. Yes, there are tons of music documentary videos, but reading people's stories in their own words provides a richness that just isn't there in video.

Watch and listen:

Study those who came before you in your primary genre, in its ancestral genres, and in music thoroughly different from your own. Knowing the context in which you're creating gives you a broader perspective, which translates into greater insight and depth of understanding in your playing and in your compositions. Young artists in traditional genres learn early to "respect your elders" and study the greats of blues, jazz, country, gospel, etc. Not all genres have this imperative built into their culture, though, so you might have to take the initiative to find and learn your history. Here's a worthwhile digital rabbit hole: Search on "music genre tree" and enjoy the gorgeous image results.

Do non-music stuff:

Spend some time on activities outside of music that broaden your creative thinking; that incorporate elements of rhythm in a different way, like painting or dancing; or that just make you happy.

SECTION 3: SYSTEMS & TOOLS

As I said way back in the beginning of Section 1, there is a difference between getting organized and being organized.

Think of the old TV shows "The Six Million Dollar Man" and "The Bionic Woman." (If you've never seen them, check out their intro sequences on YouTube.) Two people undergo complicated surgeries that give them superpowers, but the procedures and recovery take a lot of time, and even after the bulk of the work is done, they still need regular maintenance and sometimes repairs or the systems will eventually break down.

For you, getting organized is like the surgery and recovery phase, and being organized—your ultimate goal—is repairs and maintenance: everything you will do for the rest of your life to stay organized. Maintenance isn't hard; repairs aren't even hard once you really understand how your systems work. It's mostly extremely minor, like tuning, and sometimes a little more involved, like replacing worn strings or drum heads. Your organizational systems are another set of instruments that you care for in the same way.

Getting organized, like learning to sing or play, is the time-consuming and difficult part, but it will last forever if you keep it up.

In your case, though, you won't have a team of government scientists to do your upkeep: You need to learn to do it yourself. This is why I'm teaching you how to be organized—how to develop your own systems—not just giving you tips and tricks to get you fleetingly organized. This is as close as I can get to making you bionic.

CHAPTER 13:

FOUNDATIONAL TOOLS & TASKS

Pick anything in my life and ask if I have a system for it, and the answer will be yes. I have who knows how many systems—probably hundreds—but here's the key: They're all variations on a handful of basic concepts and universal tools. At the same time, as much as possible each system functions autonomously; it's not contingent on one or more other systems in order for it to work.

In this chapter, I'll show you some tools that are easily adapted for many purposes. These make multiple appearances throughout the book, both in conceptual form and in the sample tools and templates in the next chapter. We'll also go over the most basic, foundational tasks that you need to do regularly in order to keep your career on track.

Multi- vs. Single-Purpose Tools

From time to time, you might need a very specific tool that can only do one thing. But most of the time, multipurpose tools will be the better choice.

Say you have some theremin on a song on your new album. It was a cool thing to do in the studio, but it probably wouldn't make sense to take a theremin player with you on tour when your keyboardist can approximate that sound or include playback of that isolated track during live performances. The same logic applies to organizational tools: Don't invest money, space, or time in a single-purpose tool when a multipurpose one can do the job.

Your smartphone is a great example of a multipurpose tool. With it you can not only make phone calls but also send every type of message, do every web-based function, send and receive payments, take photos and videos, play and record music, tune your instrument, accompany yourself with pre-recorded tracks or improvisational loops, and on and on. In contrast, your house key is an example of a single-purpose yet essential tool. (Unless you have a house alarm that lets you unlock your door with your smartphone.)

The worst-case scenario with single-purpose tools is when you have more than one that does the same thing, and you use them all but only partially. If you use more than one calendar (e.g. a shared Google band calendar + your personal calendar + a printed calendar from work), appointments get missed. If you use more than one task system (e.g. an app for some to-dos + a paper list for other to-dos + calendar entries for to-dos you mean to do on a certain day), inevitably, tasks get missed. This redundancy of functionality makes you less organized, not more.

How to decide which tool to stick with? Put your effort into the one you're most likely to actually use. If the problem has been that each tool has some features the others don't, commit to the tool that has the features you value most and create workarounds for the elements you like from the others. If you aspire to use a task app but you find yourself jotting notes on paper instead of taking the time to open the app, choose to either a) commit to developing the self-discipline to use the app every time, or b) scrap the app, make peace with the limitations of paper, and embrace it as the system that works best for you.

Store-Bought vs. Self-Made Tools

This is similar to the concept of internally vs. externally controlled time from Chapter 1. Store-bought tools are limited in how much you can customize them to your precise purpose. Tools you make yourself will be a better fit for your needs, but you might not know how to create exactly what you want. Customizability is the never-ending tension between store-bought vs. self-made, for the organization of objects but most especially of information: data, time, and thoughts.

Paper filing systems and planners are common examples of systems you can either build from scratch or adapt from a kit. Digital systems are trickier because, unless you know computer programming, you can't reconfigure an app or program to work for you as easily as adding or removing paper pages. However, there are a few basic frameworks upon which most info-organizing tools are built, and once you're aware of them, you'll often be able to construct your own tools vs. needing a specialized app or program. Most systems for organizing information fit into one of these categories:

Containers:

Like an empty box for objects, this is simply a place to keep some information together. The information within it can be arranged however you want—in lists, in subgroups, randomly. A paper or digital sheet or notebook is a container.

Containers can also contain items formatted in any of the other categories. This book is a container which holds notes, lists, checklists, tables, spreadsheets, and one pretty cool mind map.

Checklists:

A checklist is more than just a list. It's not only for reference or information, but also drives the steps of a task or project. It doesn't have to have actual checkboxes and you don't have to actually check things off as you use it—the difference is in its purpose, not so much its format. A list of all the songs you've written is just a list, but a setlist is a checklist. There are other examples in the next chapter.

Checklists are valuable as memory prompts. They ensure you won't forget a step or vary from a routine that has been proven successful in the past or that others are counting on you to do a certain way. They're helpful even for sequences that you've performed hundreds of times because they keep you from missing a step if you're distracted or zoned out for whatever reason.

Tables:

Tables present information in a visual format that makes the relationships among the pieces of information easier to see. Headings above each column and to the left of each row indicate commonalities among the data within them. A simple monthly calendar grid is a table: You enter an appointment in one of the boxes and can now see that item in the context of all other appointments on that exact date, all appointments on that day of the week, and all appointments in the same week and month.

Spreadsheets:

Like tables, spreadsheets present data in a grid layout that shows the relationships among the data across columns and rows. Spreadsheets allow for easy sorting by those columns and rows, and they're ideal for tracking counts of various categories of data, such as merch sales and show attendance. They can be programmed to perform automatic calculations, but they can also be simply a compact format for collecting data for reference.

If you're not used to working with spreadsheets, let alone creating them, they're probably as intimidating to you as song charts are to me. The difference between us is that you can learn in a few minutes how to make a spreadsheet, but it would take me years to learn how to chart a song by ear.

You'll find several sample spreadsheet-formatted tracking documents in the next chapter.

Mind maps:

If you're cringing at all of this left-brained, linear, columns-and-rows business, here's a different type of tool to smooth out all those edges. Mind-mapping is great for brainstorming new ideas and seeing connections among them. Some people use it for the first draft of a concept and then convert it to something more structured; others keep their running notes in mind-map form all the way through.

A mind map looks more like natural doodling than top-to-bottom, left-to-right sequencing. Here's the basic flow of mind-mapping (and there's a sample in Chapter 14):

Write a thought anywhere on a blank sheet, then circle it and write related ideas around it, like moons orbiting a planet. Draw lines from the moons back to the planet to show the connections. When you think of a different planet, write it somewhere else on the page and give it moons if it has any.

If you were to reconfigure a mind map into a linear format, it would look like an outline with primary, secondary, and perhaps tertiary levels, like the bulleted lists throughout this book. There are apps to create mind maps (and some do allow you to toggle between circles and outlines), but personally I find that the act of putting pen to paper is what gives mind-mapping its creative value.

•

You have options for both store-bought and self-made tools in each of the above categories. Sometimes a store-bought, pre-fab app, software package, or template will be the right thing for you, but I encourage you to get into the groove of making your own. Over time, you'll find that you can usually whip up a checklist or spreadsheet to address any new data organization challenge that comes your way.

Let's zoom back out from a detailed view of data organization and look at some fundamental tools you need in both the physical and the digital realms.

Your Foundational Toolkit

Here are some basics every DIY musician needs these days. You'll probably think of more items that are essential for you.

Equipment:

Aside from your instruments and related music gear, there really isn't much you need in the way of physical tools, but here are a few necessities:

- Computer with internet: Take your pick of a laptop or desktop and Mac or PC, but it needs to be an actual computer. Relying on your smartphone or a tablet is too limiting. A printer will be helpful but not absolutely essential; a scanner is unnecessary for most people now, especially if you're using your phone camera to "scan" documents (see Chapter 2).
- Smartphone: Necessary in addition to a computer to do all of the mobile, in-the-moment things you need to do.
- Backup charger: I have one from OrigAudio that has multiple connectors to charge iPhones, Androids, and anything with a full USB or mini-USB charger. It has saved the day for many merch tables and live streams, and it gets me through every festival.
- Credit card reader: A rare example of a single-purpose tool that you really do need. As of this writing, we still need a device to take credit card payments with a smartphone. Swipers that plug into the headphone jack are on their way out (as are headphone jacks) and wifi chip readers are becoming the required standard. (With some apps, you can manually type in the card number, but you will pay higher rates, so it's better to use the device whenever possible.) This reader device will pair with the merchant account you choose from the digital tools list coming up next.

Digital tools:

There are a few foundational computer programs and apps that you will use for multiple purposes, and also some that only have one job, but that job is mission-critical:

- Something for notes, checklists, and tables: You need this to create basic documents which you can print or save as PDFs. Microsoft Word (either the hard-drive-installed software or the cloud version within Microsoft Office Online) or Google Docs (cloud-based and free) are common examples.
- Something for spreadsheets: They're not just for accounting. Spreadsheets are my favorite for making tracking documents and tables of information. You don't have to use the formulas to get plenty of functionality out of these. Microsoft Excel or Google Sheets are common spreadsheet programs/apps.
- Something for basic graphic design: You need this for making show posters, social media infographics, and the like. Microsoft Publisher is great for this, but if you don't already have it or something similar that came bundled with your computer, there are plenty of free sites and apps that give you similar functionality.
- A calendar app: Google Calendar works fine for most of the musicians and other businesspeople I know. It's easy to make your own personal calendar and set it to appear with other calendars you're subscribed to in a custom shared view that only you can see, and it synchronizes easily from computer web interface to mobile app. Note: If you really, truly must have a paper calendar, stick with what you require. If you have bandmates with whom you have to share a gig calendar, perhaps one of them can create and maintain a Google calendar that everyone else can use. You'll still need to look at that calendar, but you can copy the dates from it into your paper system.
- An email app: Choose something you can access easily from both your computer and your phone. Gmail is the clear favorite with everyone I know in all walks of life. Similar to Google Calendar and its multi-calendar view, you can set Gmail to receive all of your emails from

multiple addresses.

- A bulk emailing platform: If you use your individual email account for mailings to your fan email list, you'll get blacklisted as a spammer. You need a platform like MailChimp or Constant Contact to send out that type of bulk email. MailChimp is currently free up to 2,000 addresses in your database.

- A credit card merchant account or other mobile payment system: Square and PayPal are popular, easy, and trusted by customers. Be prepared for times when you can't get enough signal to run cards, either because you're out of cell range or you're in an old, solidly built venue (love ya, Continental Club in Austin, TX). You might have to go cash-only on those nights.

- A website platform: If you opt to build your own website, choose a platform in line with your levels of skill and patience. WordPress and Squarespace are adequate for most people. There are also services that build sites specifically for musicians. If you hire out the initial build, make sure you are given access and instructions to update the site yourself. Adding show dates, music links, and new photos are all super-basic functions that you don't need to pay a web developer to do.

- A cloud storage spot: You can keep your files on your hard drive, but if your computer is stolen, your work is gone. Most people are at least backing up their files to the cloud, and many are using cloud storage as their main file repository. Sites like Google Drive and Dropbox give you a limited amount of space for free, or more for a monthly fee. Check for free space bundled with subscriptions you already have, such as Amazon Prime or OneDrive with Microsoft Office Online. If you use more than one cloud site, keep a list of them so you remember what you have available and which files are where.

- A file-sharing system: Music, video, and high-res photo files will often be larger than email attachment size limits, so you need another way to share them. As with file storage, sharing is also much easier in the cloud. Check out the sharing procedures for your storage sites, or use a site like WeTransfer which allows you to send up to 2GB at a time for free.

- Social media accounts: The basics as of this writing are a Facebook page and Twitter and Instagram accounts. Refer back to Chapter 11 for the breakdown of why you need social media and what to do with it.

Things You Need to Do Every Day

Here we are at the nitty gritty. This is what being organized looks like day-to-day. It's not fancy or exciting. Every once in a while, you might look around and realize that things are running smoothly and life is better this way, but that's about as exhilarating as it gets. People often think that being organized is life in the fast lane, but it's actually more like living on a farm: steady, rhythmic, quietly satisfying, and it gives back exactly what you put in.

Here's how you keep this peaceful party going:

Check and respond to messages:

Look at/listen to voicemail, email, texts, and social media direct messages at least once a day. Aim to respond to every message within 24 hours, even when you're on tour. If the message response requires info that you don't have, let the person know you're checking on it and will get back to them. Even if it's a simple "Checking—hold please," that's better than leaving people hanging.

When messages require research or follow-up, don't just reset them as unread or leave them sitting there. Make an item in your task system or to-do list for each one so you'll be prompted to complete them.

Check your calendar:

If it's the beginning of the day, check it to get oriented to today's appointments. If it's the end of the day, look at tomorrow to prepare for those appointments. Also have a look at the rest of the week so nothing sneaks up on you. If you're using more than one calendar and they're not all integrated into one view, you'll have to check each one separately.

Look at your to-do list:

At least look at it. Even if your day is now over, it was a lost cause, and all you can do is move your deadlines ahead one day, at least do that. You need to stay in touch with this list and keep yourself in the habit of using this system.

When you have the energy to do more, give the list more than just a basic skim. Check off items completed, delete items no longer needed, add new items if you have any, adjust deadlines, recalibrate priorities and task order, and set yourself up for a good day tomorrow.

If you're looking at your recently updated list at the beginning of your day, run with it. Don't spend much time second-guessing the things you assigned to today or the way that you prioritized—if you know you put good thought into writing this list, you now get to reap the benefits of that work and simply follow your own instructions.

Peruse your business social media:

Like and respond to comments on your posts. Also like and share at least a few followers' posts on Twitter and/or Instagram. If you interact with business contacts on your personal social media, also check on those accounts daily.

Charge your rechargeables:

Every night, plug in your phone, tablet, laptop, all Bluetooth devices (headset, credit card "chip" reader), and your rechargeable battery backup. It might help to keep all of your chargers and cables together on the same power strip so you can easily spot an empty cord and go retrieve the device that should be on it.

Sleep, eat, and hydrate:

There's a lot more to self-care than this, but these are the bare basics. Don't go an entire night without sleep or an entire day without any food or water. (Yeah, I know, it might still happen in the midst of some unpreventable crisis. But if you can avoid it with organization, do.)

Things You Need to Do at Least Weekly

You don't have to zoom out from your present focus every day, but you do need to do it regularly. Weekly is a good pace to try initially. See if it works for you as a routine, then make it more frequent if needed (or less if you're sure you can keep from losing your grip):

Practice your music:

This might need to be daily. I defer to you to know what's best for your creative tasks. See Chapter 12 for more on artistic growth.

Review your big picture:

Get reoriented to your long-term goals. How are you tracking toward them? Still working the plan? Or did the plan require a change recently? Does your big picture need updating?

Update your social media posting plan:

Synchronize with your show calendar and other time-specific items you want to post about next week. Plug tasks into your to-do system to make these posts.

Assess your progress:

What did you get done this week? Where are you with booking outreach, promotion for upcoming events, or songwriting? Focus on the positives—this is not a weekly exercise in self-punishment. What can you do to set yourself up for a productive next week?

Look around:

Stop all of this work-related stuff and look around at your life. Is there anything that's falling apart and needs your attention? Relationships, household, vehicle, pets, parking tickets, taxes, plane tickets home for the holidays … anything you've been putting off dealing with? How long is it going to wait?

●

And now it's Go Time. You're on your own from here. In the next chapter, to get you started with making your own tools, I've given you examples of some of the ones I've created to manage music-biz data. You're welcome to copy anything from them, but whatever you do, don't just blindly use my tools. They probably won't fit you as they are. You must add to, delete from, and change them to really make them your own.

CHAPTER 14:

SAMPLE TOOLS & TEMPLATES

With this chapter, I'm sharing sample checklists, spreadsheets, and templates that you can use to develop your own custom tools. THESE ARE JUST STARTERS! Some of these are replications of tools I'm using right now, but by the time this book is published, I will have already changed my live versions.

Tools like these are living documents. You must adapt each one for your own needs by adding, deleting, and changing parts of it until it's exactly what you need, and then changing it again when your needs change.

A word of caution about spreadsheets: If you're considering sharing live spreadsheets for everyone in the band to update, gahhhh don't!

OK, just kidding. Kind of. Spreadsheets can be used as tables, without any fancy behind-the-scenes formatting tricks or formulas, and in that usage they're relatively hard to kill. However, those with complex formatting and formulas are easily "broken" by users who don't know how they were built or how they're meant to be used. If you find that you really like the benefits of a robust, finely tuned spreadsheet and you get into creating formulas for calculations and drop-down menus and such, it will be better to share them as read-only and ask the others to send you any updates or corrections.

ntacts & Networking

On the next page you'll find two examples of spreadsheets you can use to keep track of your general networking and of your media contacts. Working this way has advantages over keeping notes along with names, numbers, and emails in your digital Contacts app or paper phone book.

Networking Contacts:

This is an example of a spreadsheet used for tracking networking contacts. Each person's basic contact info (phone, email, mailing address, website) is in the user's digital Contacts app. You could add this info to the Notes section of each entry in your Contacts, but when you group it like this, you can easily see it in context with all of your other networking relationships. For example, you can see at a glance who is due for a check-in, who you're not yet connected with on social media, and how many people you know from a given industry or company.

Media Contacts:

You could include your media contacts in the same Networking Contacts spreadsheet, or, if that list is extensive, break out your media contacts into a separate spreadsheet like the second example. In this one, "As Of" is the date you're entering or updating the info for each person. It's useful to know how old and potentially outdated each entry is. Email and phone are good to include in your media list and also in your Contacts: This way, you have multiple emails handy to copy for press release blasts, and you have a complete list to share with hired or volunteer PR support. You also want them in your Contacts so you can grab the call when their names appear on your Caller ID.

"Market" is the city or region they cover. "Format" is print newspaper, magazine, blog, radio, TV, etc. "Pub/Air Frequency" is how often they publish or air the show. "Comm Cal?" is whether they have a Community Calendar on their website that you could post your shows to. "Most Recent Contact" is the date you last spoke to them or sent something, and "Most Recent Content" is what that most recent contact was for.

Networking Contacts and Media Contacts:

Name	Title/job	Company/ Group	Status	How We Met	FB?	LI?	Most Recent Contact	Next Check-In	Notes
[first and last]	insurance sales	State Farm	Have relationship	NBX meeting 7-14-16		y	9/1/16		See regularly at NBX.
[first and last]	owner	Nomad Sound	To approach-no link	Haven't yet.			8/23/16	Wed 09/07/16	Sent FB message.
[first and last]	?	City music office	Developing	AMF mixer 8-24-16	y	y	8/24/16	Tue 08/30/16	Said he's heard of us. Having coffee 8/30.
[first and last]	bartender	Stay Gold	Have relationship	Friends for a while	y			Sun 09/04/16	Said she would intro me to booker.
[first and last]	booker	Stay Gold	To approach-have a link	Haven't yet.					Waiting for intro from [bartender]. Then move this entry to Booking Outreach

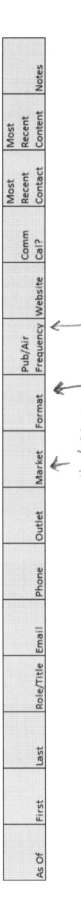

As Of	First	Last	Role/Title	Email	Phone	Outlet	Market	Format	Pub/Air Frequency	Website	Comm Cal?	Most Recent Contact	Most Recent Content	Notes

Market ← city/region they cover

Format ← mag, blog, print, radio, tv, etc.

Pub/Air Frequency ← How often they publish or air

Booking & Gig Tracking

You'll send thousands of booking pitch emails over the course of your career, so taking an organized approach will save you time, minimize stress, and optimize your follow-up effectiveness. Below are some samples of email wording, followed by a tracking document you can use to keep yourself oriented to what you've done and what still needs doing.

Booking pitch sample emails:

Here are a few examples of email verbiage for booking outreach. There is no good reason to write a new and different email every time—it's fine to send 20 emails with the same wording, each addressed to a different talent buyer. Come up with templates appropriate for each type of pitch, written in your own voice, and with your key links already included, and copy them into a blank email to send individually to each recipient.

If you have a specific name in the salutation, be sure to replace it in each email. Mike will be highly unimpressed to receive an email that opens with "Hi Lucy!"

Here's an example for a nontraditional venue (a place where live music happens but they're not a music venue per se). This place does not have an online calendar of upcoming shows, so you'll have to go with the otherwise ill-advised request for "any openings." Replace the portions in brackets with specifics about your act and venue's audience. If you know the booker's name, include it in the subject ("For Lisa: Booking live music?") and the salutation ("Hello Lisa!"):

Subject: Booking live music?

Hello! I'm a local musician interested in performing live at your establishment, either as background music for your guests or as a featured artist. I [am a vocalist/play acoustic guitar/piano/violin/etc.] and have a repertoire of music enjoyable for a [dinner/lounge/happy hour] audience. Do you have any openings in your schedule at this time?

Thank you!

[Name]
[Phone]
[website or social media page link]

Here's an example for a traditional venue. Try to find the booker's name (on the venue website or Indie on the Move, or via your networking contacts) and check their calendar of upcoming shows to ask for specific dates:

Subject: [Genre] [band name] for [date]?

Hello [booker name]! [Genre] [band name] checking interest/avail for [date]. Our EPK is at [link]. Thanks!

[Name]
[Phone]
[website or social media page link]

If you're uncomfortable being this succinct, go ahead and use full sentences, paragraph breaks, or other courtesies, but be aware that talent buyers frequently cite lengthy booking pitch emails as a source of annoyance.

If you want to include a sentence describing your band or sound, make it objectively descriptive ("We're an alt-rock 5-piece with a repertoire of 90 minutes of originals and 3 hours of covers"), not salesy ("I guarantee you'll love us!"). If applicable, you can add further details such as:

- "Our average draw in [name of venue's town] is [a real number; don't lie]."
- "We're touring through and would need this particular date."
- "We're open to a support slot if needed."
- "We're touring behind a new album."

Don't mention money in your initial pitch. Wait for a reply before you go there.

Follow-ups:

If you've waited a week or more and haven't gotten a reply to your initial pitch (which is typical), forward your original email to the talent buyer with a very brief, very courteous note in the new email—something like, "Hi [name], just bringing this back around. Thanks so much!"

Consider sending this email on a different day of the week and/or at a different time of day. Your first one might have arrived at a peak time for this person and gotten buried. Don't add more info to plead your case unless there is some legitimately significant news to report, such as winning an impressive prize or getting booked to a big festival lineup.

If you still get no response, try a follow-up call unless the venue has indicated somewhere (website, social media, IOTM) that email is the only acceptable method for booking outreach. Try calling in the early afternoon to avoid getting voicemail if s/he is still sleeping and to catch him or her before the busyness of the evening. Even talent buyers who aren't onsite with a particular venue tend to be busy with last-minute issues later in the day or at night.

Booking Outreach Tracker:

Here's a spreadsheet for monitoring the basics of your booking outreach. You might want to add more columns depending on your needs, such as whether or not they have a PA or backline, the date you last played, whether they have a house photographer, etc.

Compare this to the info in the Master Schedule up next. Does it make sense for you to combine these into one sheet, with the prospects you're working on entered in rows below the confirmed dates in the Master Schedule, or do you need to keep your booking prospects separate to prevent visual overwhelm?

Notice that this example is sorted alphabetically by city. You could also sort it by state, capacity, or age to facilitate tour planning.

"Next Follow Up On" is the date you intend to reach out again if you haven't heard back. Deciding what this date should be—how long to wait—is debatable, but I allow at least a week. Having said that, I start with a planned timeline but deviate from it if I feel like the situation calls for it, similar to how you might change your performance based on the audience's response.

The function I consider most essential here is keeping track of how many times you've circled back on the same request. In this example, you can enter them as running commentary in the notes section, or if you prefer you could make columns for 1st attempt, 2nd attempt, etc. Much of the anxiety of booking outreach comes from wondering if you're being too aggressive or not aggressive enough, trying to decide when to give up on a prospect, or having that nagging feeling that you've forgotten something. All of those worries are eased when you have the details of your outreach right in front of you.

Booking Outreach Tracker:

Venue	City	State	Capacity	Age	Website	Booking Contact Name	Email	Phone	Initial Email Sent	Next Follow Up On	Notes
[venue name]	Ann Arbor	MI	100	21+	www....	Rick	booking@...	555-...	[date]	[date]	Each attempt, reply, feedback received, etc.
[venue name]	Austin	TX	300		www....		booking@...	555-...	[date]	[date]	
[venue name]	Austin	TX	100	21+	www....		booking@...	555-...	[date]	[date]	
[venue name]	Austin	TX	200	21+	www....		booking@...	555-...	[date]	[date]	
[venue name]	Austin	TX	400	Varies	www....	David	booking@...	555-...	[date]	[date]	
[venue name]	Dallas	TX	400		www....		booking@...	555-...	[date]	[date]	
[venue name]	Detroit	MI	250		www....		booking@...	555-...	[date]	[date]	
[venue name]	Little Rock	AR	150	21+	www....	Matt	booking@...	555-...	[date]	[date]	
[venue name]	Memphis	TN	120	All	www....	Steven	booking@...	555-...	[date]	[date]	
[venue name]	Shreveport	LA	225		www....		booking@...	555-...	[date]	[date]	
[venue name]	South Bend	IN	150	21+	www....	Ben	booking@...	555-...	[date]	[date]	
[venue name]	St. Louis	MO	300	21+	www....		booking@...	555-...	[date]	[date]	
[venue name]	Tyler	TX	280	21+	www....	see IOTM	booking@...	555-...	[date]	[date]	

Master Schedule Spreadsheet:

This one's a beast. It extends across more than 30 columns to comprehensively track the details of each performance or event. You could add even more columns for info such as which of your rotating side players were on each gig, or you could combine it with the Show Profit & Loss Tracker up next to prevent having two running lists of your gigs.

Sheets like this are both a working document for the present and future as well as an archival record of the past. They're extremely valuable for keeping details handy when you're soliciting repeat bookings and anticipating draw at shows in markets you play infrequently or which are near markets that will be new to you.

In the live version of this spreadsheet, the Event Type column is a drop-down menu with options for the type of performance, event, or related activity. Drop-downs with limited choices are useful in spreadsheets because they force you to organize your data into predefined categories vs. entering random, inconsistent language in a field. Creating drop-downs is a somewhat involved function within Excel, but once you learn it you'll have a valuable new trick.

Here are a few other notes about the rationale behind this setup:

- Column A: I add items to this sheet as soon as they're held but before they're confirmed, which could be weeks apart. I put the Confirmed? Column at the front so I can see at a glance which items are definitely a go.
- B: Notice the color info at the top of the column. Spreadsheets can be incomprehensible, even when you're practiced at looking at them. Color-coding makes it easier to make sense of what you're seeing. In my live version, I use blue and green vs. shades of gray.
- Also in B, I formatted the column to automatically expand dates to include the day of the week (e.g. I typed 3/6/15 and Excel converted it).
- C: These distinctions tell me at a glance how much and what types of PR will be needed for the event. I place travel here to account for the time it will take, and I include lodging info here to coordinate check-in times with venue load-in.
- H: You might think doors time isn't directly relevant unless you're self-producing, but it's good to be aware of it because it sometimes happens during soundcheck. You want to know when attendees will start coming in so you can have your merch setup ready and/or escape to the greenroom.
- K-U: These columns are all for PR tasks. I've found this essential to prevent missed postings and also to prevent obsessive double-triple checking. "Band cal" means it's been entered on the band calendar (whether as a hold or go). "SRBP" is Sonicbids, ReverbNation, Bandsintown, and Pollstar: I enter the letter of each as I post them, which isn't always all at the same time. Notice that private events don't go on Pollstar, but they do go on the others (as Private Event with city but no street address) to reinforce the band's popularity. "PR Advance" and "Press Advance" have formulas that automatically calculate based on the event date in column B. "Event Name" is a festival name, for example.
- V-X: This is useful to track for future shows at the same venue or festival and for comparison to similar gigs. You can add further detail in Y-AC, which will be especially important when you're self-producing the show.
- AD-AH: These aren't used for every show, so I keep them at the far right and out of the way of the most active details.

Master Schedule Spreadsheet (pasted in two sections):

Lt gray = no overnight
Dk gray = road
White = info

	A	B	C	D	E	F	G	H	I	J	K	L	M	N	O	P	Q	R	S	T	U	V
	Conf irmed?	Date	Event Type	Venue	City	State in	Call Time/ Load In	Doors	Perf Times	Sets/ Length	Band cal	Social Media Cal	Song kick	SRBP	Do 512	On Venue Cal?	FB Event?	Pos-ter? Add to cals	PR Advance 6-wks	Press Advance 3-wks	Advance Event Name	Role
2		Friday, March 6, 2015	**Drive**	3.75 hrs																		
3	y	Friday, March 6, 2015	Perf-Public	[venue nam	[city]	[st]	5p	7p	9p-12a	2 75s	y	y	y	SRBP	n	y	y-venu		1/23/15	2/13/15		Sole
4		Friday, March 6, 2015	**Lodging**	[hotel name]																		
5		Saturday, March 7, 2015	**Drive**	1.5 hrs																		
6	y	Saturday, March 7, 2015	Perf-Public	[venue nam	[city]	[st]	4-7p	7p	11p-12:15a	1 75	y	y	y	SRBP	n	y	y		1/24/15	2/14/15		Headliner
7		Saturday, March 7, 2015	**Lodging**	[hotel name]																		
8		Sunday, March 8, 2015	**Drive**	1.75 hrs																		
9	y	Sunday, March 8, 2015	Perf-Public	[venue nam	[city]	[st]	3p	5p	8-9p	1 60	y	y	y	SRBP	n	y	y (venu		1/25/15	2/15/15		Headliner
10		Sunday, March 8, 2015	**Lodging**	[hotel name]																		
11	y	Monday, March 9, 2015	Recording-Aud	studio nam	[city]	[st]	9a				y	y	n	n	n	n	n					
12	y	Tuesday, March 10, 2015	Recording-Aud	studio nam	[city]	[st]	9a				y	y	n	n	n	n	n					
13		Tuesday, March 10, 2015	**Drive**	5 hrs																		
14		Tuesday, March 10, 2015	**Lodging**	[hotel nam Note: late check-in																		
15	y	Wednesday, March 11, 2015	Recording-Aud	studio nam	[city]	[st]	10a				y	y	n	n	n	n	n					
16	y	Thursday, March 12, 2015	Recording-Aud	studio nam	[city]	[st]	10a				y	y	n	n	n	n	n					
17	y	Friday, March 13, 2015	Perf-Public	[venue nam	[city]	[st]	6:30p	8p	10p-12:15a	2 60s	y	y	y	SRBP	n	n	y		1/30/15	2/20/15		Headliner
18		Saturday, March 14, 2015	**Drive**	7 hrs																		
19	y	Friday, March 20, 2015	Perf-Public	[venue nam	[city]	[st]	11a-12p	1p	1-4p	3 50s	y	y	y	SRBP	y	n	n					Headliner
20	y	Saturday, March 21, 2015	Perf-Public	[venue nam	[city]	[st]	7p	8p	10-10:45p	1 45	y	y	y	SRBP	y	y	n					Dir supp
21	y	Saturday, March 28, 2015	Perf-Public	[venue nam	[city]	[st]	6:30p	8p	9:30p-12:15	2 75s	y	y	y	SRBP	n	y	y					Sole
22	y	Tuesday, March 31, 2015	Perf-Private-Bus	[location]	[city]	[st]	4p	5p	6-8p	2 55s	y	y	y	SRB	n	y	n					Sole
23	y	Saturday, April 4, 2015	Perf-Public	[venue nam	[city]	[st]	2-4p	7p	9:30p	1 90	y	y	y	SRBP	n	y	y		2/21/15	3/14/15		Dir supp
24	y	Sunday, April 5, 2015	Perf-Public	[venue nam	[city]	[st]	10p	7p	11:30p-12:3	1 60	y	y	y	SRBP	venu	y	n					Headliner

W	X	Y	Z	AA	AB	AC	AD	AE	AF	AG	AH
Contact pers	Fee/Guar.	Prod. Costs	Support Acts	Split	Tix Price	Notes	Print/Web Media	Commercial Radio	Commercial TV	University Radio	University Student Life

Show Profit & Loss Tracker:

Here's an excerpt from a spreadsheet for tracking revenue and expenses by event. In this example, the band has a weekly Tuesday night residency, plays some club gigs, and also gets an occasional private gig. They have a band fund, which is used for expenses like travel out of town, paid promotion, and merch orders, and they have agreements in place about how merch and tip money is handled and how player payouts are calculated (equal split with band fund "extra man").

You can create this by hand in a ledger or as a table in Word or Google Docs, or (as shown here) a spreadsheet in Excel or Google Sheets where you can create formulas to do the math for you. You might also want to add a column titled Draw for tracking attendance at each show. The live version of this spreadsheet contains formulas that automagically perform the calculations.

If you're absolutely fearless and immune to overwhelm in Excel, you could just add these columns into the Master Schedule tracker and have one enormous worksheet for all information pertaining to each show. Keep in mind that it will be unprintable because it will extend across so many columns, but if that's how your mind works, go for it.

Note: These numbers are just examples, not necessarily averages or suggestions of what you should be getting paid.

Show Profit & Loss Tracker:

Date	Event	Venue	Show Payout	Merch Sales	Tips	Gross Revenue	Player Payouts	Paid Promo	Merch Comps	Other Exps	Total Net Revenue	Notes
9/20/2016	Residency	Hotel Fancypants	$150	$20	$37	$207	$150	$0	$0	$0	$57	Duo; split payout, put merch & tips in band fund
9/24/2016	Band A direct support	Club Semi-Hip	$300	$180	$0	$480	$300	$50	$20	$0	$110	4-pc; split payout, exps out of merch, net to band fund
10/1/2016	Wedding	Hall of Lurv	$1,000	$0	$0	$1,000	$750	$0	$40	$0	$210	5-pc; $150 each; net to band fund

Tour Budget Worksheet:

The most important element of tour budgeting is realistic expectations. You should earn some money from shows and merch sales, but overall, touring is more likely to be a marketing expense than a revenue generator. Once you have an established route with pockets of fans in a circuit of towns beyond your home base, you can expect to actually turn a profit. However, if the purpose of the tour is to expand your audience in areas where you are relatively unknown, you can consider it a great success if you break even.

Your first few tours will likely be net expenses, because they'll be all about creating a presence in new markets. Soon enough, though, you'll have reliable draw in those towns, which will enable you to absorb the expense of expanding your established route with one or two new towns each time you head out. Even then, your goal might still be to break even, with the profit from your growing draw at your established stops offsetting the net losses from your first time playing new towns.

The example on the next page shows a very basic budgeting template. Remember, this is just a sample to get you thinking. Add lines to it for expenses or income sources not shown here. The more comprehensive, the better: Try to anticipate as much as you possibly can.

One difference with this template vs. others you might find online (and I encourage you to search the web for more examples) is that I've subdivided income and expenses into fixed and variable items. This helps you to isolate the areas where you're taking risks and give them the attention they need. If you roll guaranteed income in with anticipated or hoped-for income, you might perceive your overall risk to be less than it actually is, and that doesn't allow you to make a truly informed choice about whether you can afford what you're planning to do.

Here are some further notes about this example:

- This is a 4-person band on a 10-day tour. The tour is a combo of established and new markets, so they have a mix of guarantees vs. door deals. They have free lodging (friends' and fans' couches) on nights 1, 2, 4, and 6, and night 10 is close enough to drive home after the gig.
- Fixed expenses are items for which you know the price in advance (e.g. van rental) and also items for which you can set a limit (e.g. per diem). Variable expenses are items like gasoline for which you have no choice but to pay whatever it costs when you get there. There are many other expenses that you might need to add, such as insurance or gear rental.
- "Per diem" is business-speak for daily allowance. It's a set amount of money given to each person to cover or offset personal expenses like meals and laundry. This band has guaranteed each member $15 per day; for anything more than that, they're spending their own money.
- These guys are going sardine-style with a single 2-queen room per night, and whenever possible they've booked their room at motels that include a free breakfast.
- Projecting gasoline expense is a bit unnerving, especially if you're using an unfamiliar rental van and have to guess how many miles per gallon you'll get. The example here is based on 10 miles per gallon, $2.30 per gallon, and 3,200 miles total.
- This band has agreed to share the risk and split the profit (if there is one) evenly at the end. It is imperative that you discuss this well in advance, before you've confirmed any bookings, because disagreement here can doom the tour. Be aware that many musicians want to be paid more for a tour than for home gigs because they have to be away from their day jobs.

Tour Budget Worksheet:

Fixed Income	
Night 1 (Thurs) guar	$300
Night 2 (Fri) guar	$400
Night 3 (Sat) guar	$500
Night 7 (Wed.; private event) guar	$700
Night 10 (Sat.) guar	$500
Variable Income (estimates)	
Night 4 (Sun) house concert	$150
Night 5 (Mon) bar split	$100
Night 6 (Tues) door split	$100
Night 8 (Thurs) door split	$300
Night 9 (Fri) door split	$400
Merch (avg $100/night)	$1,000
Fixed Expenses	
Per diem ($15/day per member)	-$600
Van rental	-$1,200
Motel nights 3, 5, 7, 8, 9	-$200
Facebook ads	-$300
Posters to 8 venues	-$200
Variable Expenses (estimates)	
Gasoline	-$736
Profit	$1,214
Band payout (25% per member)	$303.50

Marketing & Promotion

Here are three tools that work well together. The Social Media Calendar helps you to plan and pace your posts across all platforms, ensuring you're giving heavy attention to events as appropriate and filling in with project-level promo to prevent long silences between events. The Promo Mind Map frees you to plot your initial event strategy with some creative brainstorming. The Event Promotion Grid lets you plan your activities and timing around each of your shows or events, coordinating with and expanding the details of the Social Media Calendar.

Social Media Calendar:

First up, on the next page is an example of a social media calendar made with a spreadsheet app. This band aims for daily activity on their Facebook page, Twitter, and Instagram, weekly on their YouTube channel, and at least monthly with their newsletter/email list.

The main items are noted here, and there are also daily or near-daily interactions such as liking, retweeting, and reposting followers' posts, posts the band is tagged in, show previews, media mentions, and so on. They are steadily active all week, but they post even more heavily right before and right after shows.

This is a relatively busy social media presence. If you don't have the person-power to keep up this pace, go for fewer posts or fewer platforms. Just make sure that your shows are always well-promoted (see the Event Promotion Grid) and that you respond to comments on whatever you post.

Social Media Calendar:

WK OF MON	M	T	W	Th	F	Sa	Su
6/1/15					**6/5-[venue/event]**	**6/6-[venue/event]**	
FB	Last week show pix/thx	Weekend show previews	Big show tease	Big show announcement	Show tomorrow	Show last night thanks	Show last night thanks
FB	[Create events for shows added (last week)]		#Bandlife pic		Show tonight	Show tonight	
FB	Early notice-future shows	Share article	Share fan post or pic		At venue	At venue	
Twitter	#MusicMonday	#Bandlife pic	Share article	Show tomorrow	Show tomorrow	Show last night thanks	Show last night thanks
Twitter	Early notice-future shows				Show tonight	Show tonight	
Twitter					At venue	At venue	
Instagram		#BestFans pic repost	#Bandlife pic	Best of last week		At venue	Fan last night show pic
YouTube		Monthly update					
Newsletter							
6/8/15						**6/13-[venue/event]**	
FB	Last week show pix/thx	Weekend show previews	Share fan post or pic	#Bandlife pic	Show tomorrow	Show tonight	Show last night thanks
FB	[Create events for shows added (last week)]	Share article				At venue	
FB	Early notice-future shows						
Twitter	#MusicMonday		#Bandlife pic		#FanFriday / Show tomorrow	Show tonight	Show last night thanks
Twitter	Early notice-future shows						
Twitter						At venue	
Instagram	#Bandlife pic		#BestFans pic repost	Best of last week		At venue	
YouTube		Tour alert (Central & West TX)					
Newsletter							
6/15/15						**6/20-[venue/event]**	**21-Father's Day, [venue/event]**
FB	Last week show pix/thx	Weekend show previews	#Bandlife pic	Share article	Show tomorrow	Show tomorrow	Pix of bandmembers and dads
FB	[Create events for shows added (last week)]	Share fan post or pic				Show tonight	Show last night thx & tonight
FB	Early notice-future shows					At venue	At venue
Twitter	#MusicMonday		Share article	#Bandlife pic	#FanFriday / Show tomorrow	Show tomorrow	Show last night thx & tonight
Twitter	Early notice-future shows					Show tonight	Father's Day pix
Twitter						At venue	At venue
Instagram		#Bandlife pic	#BestFans pic repost	Best of last week		At venue	At venue
YouTube							
Newsletter							
6/22/15						**6/27-[venue/event]**	
FB	Last week show pix/thx	Weekend show previews	Share article	Share fan post or pic	Show tomorrow	Show tonight	Show last night thanks
FB	[Create events for shows added (last week)]					At venue	
FB	Early notice-future shows						
Twitter	#MusicMonday	#Bandlife pic		Share article	#FanFriday / Show tomorrow	Show tonight	Show last night thanks
Twitter	Early notice-future shows						
Twitter						At venue	
Instagram		#BestFans pic repost		Best of last week		At venue	
YouTube							
Newsletter		#BestFans pic repost					

Promo Mind Map:

Sometimes brainstorming is more easily done as doodling instead of a strait-laced table or spreadsheet. Here's an example of a mind map for initial planning of the promotion of a self-produced showcase.

Promo Mind Map:

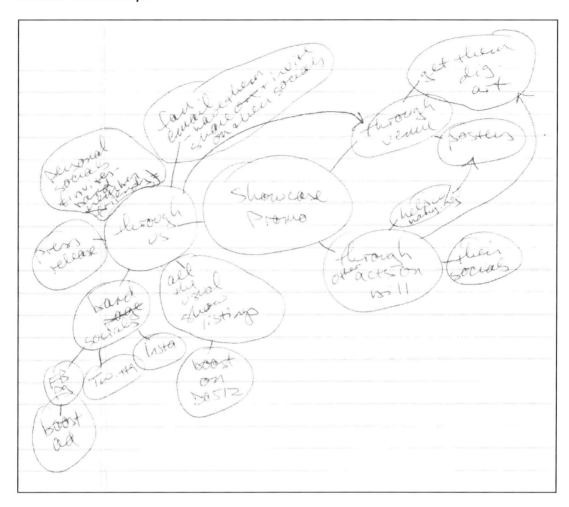

Event Promotion Grid:

Here's a way of gathering all of your promotional tasks in one view, organized by the type of task and the timeframe in which you plan to do it. The frequency of your posts on each of the social media platforms will vary depending on which is your primary.

There are many tasks not represented here, such as follow-up on any responses from media outreach, and there are presumably many more social media posts happening in addition to those related to this event. You can coordinate all of your social media posts around all of your events with a Social Media Calendar like the one shown a few pages back.

Event Promotion Grid:

	Media	Facebook Page & Event	Facebook Profiles	Twitter	Instagram	Email Newsletter	Posters	Website, Merch
8 wks	Book in-studios	Create event, share to page		Follow venue, other bands		On the Horizon to 100-mile radius	Send concept and deets to designer	Post event to website
7 wks		Update post in event						
6 wks	Press release	Update post in event & on page					Review drafts	
5 wks		Update post in event						Order event-specific merch
4 wks		Update post in event & on page	Invite friends to event	On the Horizon, tag venue		Show blurb in email to full list	Finalize design, send to printer	Reorder more standard merch if needed
3 wks		Update post in event					Drop off with venue	
2 wks		Update post in event (x2), boost event to region	Update post in event (x2)	FB event link, tag venue & other bands		Show Reminder to 100-mile radius	Post around town	
1 wk	Press alert	Update post in event (x3)	Share event, 1 wk notice	FB event link, tag venue & other bands	Event-related photo		Post more	Event scrolling banner on website
6 days		Update post in event		Event-related photo				
5 days		Update post in event, rehearsal pic on page wall		Rehearsal pic w/event link & tags	Event-related photo		Confirm venue hung posters, add more if needed	
4 days		Radio perf tmrw in event & on page		Radio perf tmrw				
3 days	Radio in-studio	Radio perf tonight in event & on page	Share event, tune in tonight for radio perf	Radio perf tonight	Radio in-studio photo	Show Reminder to 100-mile radius	Check around town, add/ uncover if needed	
2 days		Radio perf link in event & on page	Radio perf playback link	Radio perf playback link	Radio in-studio vid clip			
1 day		TV perf tmrw in event & on page	Tune in tmrw for TV perf	Tune in tmrw for TV perf				Stock merch, prep display & kit
Day of	Morning TV in-studio	TV perf link in event & on page	TV perf playback link; come out tonight	TV perf link + 2 more before, 1 immed. before, 1 after	TV in-studio photo, venue pic immed. before		Save a few from venue, sign for giveaways	Event today scrolling banner on website
Day after		Thanks & photos in event & on page	Thanks to friends	Thanks, retweets	Best event photo, reshare fan pix	Add new emails to dbase, send thx/ welcome email	Take down if needed	Inventory merch

Merch & Recordings

This section includes some sample checklists, procedures lists, and spreadsheets for keeping your merch and recordings organized—both the procedures and the inventories.

A little effort goes a long way:

It hurts my heart to see your shabby cardboard box of CDs sitting on the edge of the stage, or worse, off in an unlit corner. It's like sending your kid to school with wrinkled clothes and messy hair on picture day—come on, you love them more than this, so show it. Many bands treat merch as an afterthought and miss out on hundreds of dollars in sales per show plus all of the intangible marketing benefits that come with having an impressive merchandising display.

Getting organized with your procedures, equipment, and inventory will pay off especially well in this realm of your business. The sample tools in the following pages will get you started.

Organized recording and recordings:

Organizing your time before recording and capturing the key details of each song after it's recorded will also both save and earn you money.

As we talked about in Chapter 10, recording is expensive and stressful enough to begin with, but an organized approach can prevent it from being chaotic and financially wasteful. A well-planned, thorough pre-production process will save you time and money, and even more important, it will give you the best possible environment to set aside administrative details and immerse yourself in creativity. The sample pre-pro checklist in this section is a good template for creating your own steps and timeline.

Once they're in the can, those mastered song files are useful not only for distributing for commercial sale and streaming but also for licensing for use in films, commercials, TV shows, and more. Many consider it the fastest-growing revenue opportunity for indie artists these days, but to take advantage of it, you've got to have your catalog in order. The two tracking documents that finish this section will help you to get your recordings organized for rights management and sync licensing.

Merch Kit Checklist:

Stuff gets forgotten at home. Stuff gets taken out and used for something else. Stuff gets used up and not replenished. A checklist of what's supposed to be in the merch kit allows you to correct those situations before you head out to the gig.

This is my list when I set up a merch table as a legit merchandising area which also serves as a concierge station for the band and merch rep. Make your own list, balancing necessity or usefulness and portability/transport space.

	Equipment & Supplies:
	Merch Procedures (in plastic page protector)
	Long folding table
	Small pop-up table
	Shower curtain (waterproof, beer-proof) as tablecloth
	Large black cloth for covering table during breaks
	Heavy-duty surge strip with long (10') cord
	Folding display rack
	String lights (4), small clip-on lamp
	ClipSigns foldable hanging poles
	Wooden hangers (1 per shirt design/color)
	Tips sign and container
	Meet & Greet sign
	Merch items list/price sheet (2; in plastic page protectors)
	Large-print list of tracks on each album (2; in plastic page protectors)
	Clipboards for email list (2)
	Credit card swiper
	Cash pouch with starter change
	Blank paper (for setlists), sticky notes
	Pens (2-4)
	Sharpies (6-8; black, silver, gold)
	Mini flashlight, folding multi-tool
	Zip ties, binder clips (various sizes but at least 4 of XL)
	Empty flash drive
	Portable cellphone charger w/iOS, Android, and USB connectors
	White gaff tape
	Large safety pins, travel sewing kit
	Small mirror
	Disposable ear plugs
	Mints, gum, Tums, ibuprofen, cold/allergy meds, tissues, band-aids, sunblock, candy/snacks, hand sanitizer
	Products, Handouts, Forms to Be Printed Each Time:
	Shirts (2-3 per size/style/color per show)
	CDs (old 10 per show, new 20 per show)
	Vinyl (old 2 per show, new 5 per show)
	Stickers (big stack)
	Fan club postcards (big stack)
	Email list signup sheet (2)
	Booking business cards

Merch Procedures for Band/Staff:

Here's an easy walkthrough for running merch show to show, with or without a fan volunteer to staff the table for you. Writing down the steps in this way saves you from having to try to remember and makes it possible for any bandmember or other trusted person to jump in and help.

Without Fan Volunteer	With Fan Volunteer
Before the Show	
• Decide who's running merch tonight. • Download the sales app. • Make sure the merch kit is prepped and stocked.	• Confirm arrival time with the fan, send them the volunteer procedures (not this, the other one), add them to guest list. • Change the sales app password to something just for today.
Setting Up	
• Set up the display.	• Give the fan your cell number for panic texts.
• Log in on sales app.	• Log them in on the sales app on their phone.
• Count inventory.	• Walk them through the products, sales procedure, how to collect emails, etc.
Pre-show Sales	
• Do it if there's time between sound check and start. If not, cover the table with the black cloth and put up the "Back After Last Set" sign.	• Confirm they have what they need, then let them do it.
After the Show	
• With or without a volunteer, before you leave backstage, remind everyone to get to the merch table ASAP. If fans want to chat as soon as you hop offstage, say, "Hey, sure, walk with me!" and visit with them as you make your way to the table.	
• Get behind the table and start selling. Count on bandmates to do the schmoozing, or if you're solo, schmooze/sell as best you can.	• Let the volunteer know you're there. • Grab a Sharpie for autographing. • Stay close but not in the way of buyers.
Packing Up	
• Tally remaining inventory.	• Get inventory & cash, log them out of sales app.
• Put everything away (neatly for next time) and load out.	• Get a photo with the volunteer. Make sure you have their correct name spelling. Post to social media with a big thanks before you forget.
	• Load out after volunteer is done packing up.
	• Change the sales app password again.

Merch Procedures for Fan Volunteers:

Here's a sample instruction sheet for your fan volunteers. Create your own version to email in advance and also keep a copy in the merch kit. Notice the language is lighter & friendlier than the to-the-point internal procedures in the previous example.

Before the Show

- Download the sales app to your phone. We'll have a reader and the login info for you. Please be sure your phone is fully charged and/or bring a battery charger with you.

Setting Up

- Get familiar with the products we have with us tonight. (Use the display price sheet as a cheat sheet.)
- Get logged in on the sales app.
- Set up the display. Go ahead and be creative!
- Count and write down the number of each item on hand. (We might have already done this for you.)

Pre-show Sales

- Be ready to sell when doors open.
- Chat with folks who stop by the table. Ask whether they've seen us before. Encourage them to sign up for our email newsletter and feel free to tell them what you love about our music!
- Keep an eye on products, equipment, and the cash pouch. Most people are honest, but ya never know....
- Some fans, especially those who have seen us before, will buy things before the show. They might ask that you hold it for them until after, and that's fine – just put a note on the item and set it aside.
- If you can't get enough signal to run credit card charges, don't panic. It happens sometimes in older venues. Ask venue staff if they have wifi. If that doesn't work, text one of us to see if our phone will work better. Worst case scenario, just tell folks it'll be cash-only tonight.

During the Show

- When we hit the stage, wrap up your last transactions in progress, put away the cash and the equipment, throw the black cloth over the table, set out the "Back After the Last Set" sign, and come enjoy the show!

After the Show

- Get back to the table as quickly as you can. (Bonus points if you can stand to miss the end of the encore!)
- We'll join you as soon as possible to visit with fans and sign autographs. Please have the Sharpies ready for us.
- Sell, baby, sell! Don't worry if you get backed up – just look up once in a while at the next few people in line, smile, and thank them for waiting. It'll be fine. ☺

Packing Up

- You made it! Job well done!
- Count the number of each item remaining and compare to the pre-show count. Now we'll know how much we sold – woot!
- With your last bit of energy, please put away the remaining inventory and equipment. We'll load it out.
- Give one of us the cash and log out of the sales app. (You can now delete the app if you want, or save it for next time!)
- If we haven't done this already, please remind us to get a photo with you so we can thank you on social media!

Tour Merch Inventory:

Here's an easy way for your hometown merch person to send you on tour and get everything back in some semblance of order. All you have to do is write in the counts after each gig.

This is better than just counting everything when you return because it tells you what sold in each city. Over time, you'll be able to anticipate which towns need smaller or larger shirts, which are bigger fans of vinyl, etc. You can also use it for local shows.

You can create this as a table in Word or a spreadsheet in Excel to print and send with the merch, or you can skip the digital setup and use a ledger, graph-paper notebook, or even just hand-drawn columns on a legal pad.

Tour Merch Inventory:

	Start	Fri 12/5 Count Out	Sat 12/6 Count Out	Tues 12/9 Count Out	Thurs 12/11 Count Out	Fri 12/12 Count Out	Sat 12/13 Count Out
Album 1 CD	40						
Album 2 CD	40						
Album 2 Vinyl	10						
Album 3 CD	60						
Album 3 Vinyl	25						
Shirts:							
Logo Black S	2						
Logo White S	2						
Logo Black M	3						
Logo White M	3						
Logo Black L	3						
Logo White L	3						
Logo Black XL	3						
Logo White XL	3						
Logo Black 2X	1						
Logo White 2X	1						
Album Gray S	4						
Album Blue S	4						
Album Gray M	8						
Album Blue M	8						
Album Gray L	8						
Album Blue L	8						
Album Gray XL	8						
Album Blue XL	8						
Album Gray 2X	3						
Album Blue 2X	3						

Note: These Start counts are just an example. Yours will depend on the specifics of your act and the shows you're preparing for. Try to take just enough not to miss any sales but not so much that it's a burden to haul.

Pre-Production Checklist:

Review the points in Chapter 10, then use this worksheet as a template to create your own pre-pro checklist. Skim all of the tasks listed here and make any additions you need, determine how much time it will take to complete each one, and work backwards from your recording start date to fill in the dates you'll be working on each step. If you discover that you should have started pre-production several weeks ago or more, consider whether you should push back recording until you can be fully prepared.

Pre-Production Checklist:

Start Date	Time Needed	Administrative Pre-Pro Steps (running concurrently with creative steps below)
		Reach out to studios you're interested in. Get rates and learn details about engineering (e.g. house vs. contracted), house equipment/gear available for your use, how far in advance they book, and other specs affecting your decision. If necessary, ask for their help in estimating how much time you will need. Determine your first- and second-choice studios.
		If separate from studios, reach out to engineers and producers. Consider factors such as availability, experience with similar music, and willingness to be as collaborative or as hands-off as you prefer. Get their philosophy on brick-by-brick vs. song-a-day. Discuss options for recording based on your distribution media choices (digital, CD, vinyl). Learn whether fees are by the hour or the song and whether payment is cash, producer points, or both. Determine your first and second choices.
		Decide how many songs you will record in this round, i.e. whether you're doing an album, EP, or one or more singles. Consider studio and production costs to determine how many songs/how much time you can afford.
		Set your budget. Decide in advance how much you will spend, and know how much of that money you already have vs. how much you still need to acquire and by what dates. Determine how each player will be compensated and also who will receive songwriting percentages and how they will be divided. Draft work-for-hire agreements if needed.
		Choose your target recording dates. Enter them at the bottom of this checklist and calculate the remaining steps by working backwards from the recording start date.
		Decide which songs will be recorded in this round. Set timeline to complete studio arrangements of those songs.
		Decide which band members will be recording plus any studio or guest players you want to include. Check their availability and put tentative holds on their time. Arrange for backups to be on call if necessary.
		Call back your first-choice studio, producer, and engineer and place tentative holds on your target dates. Move on to your second choices if necessary.
		Confirm dates with the studio, engineer, producer, and all players. Get all contracts and performer agreements signed. Send follow-up emails to all reiterating the confirmed dates.
		Send final schedule including each person's arrival times. Remind everyone to perform maintenance on their instruments if needed before arriving for the first session.
Start Date	Time Needed	Creative Pre-Pro Steps (running concurrently with admin steps above)
		Finish the songs. Make up your mind(s) about every element of each song, including the tempo you want to record at (which might differ from how you play it live).
		Distribute the songs for individual practice and group rehearsal prep. Emphasize the importance of learning these exact arrangements.
		First group rehearsal. Rehearse in the same way you will be recording, e.g. individually in isolation, playing to a click track only, playing with scratch vocals, etc. Confirm that everyone has learned and is able to perform their parts reliably.
		Adjust arrangements, if desired, based on results of first rehearsal. Distribute changes to everyone.
		Schedule and complete additional group and section rehearsals. If working with an outside producer, consider having him/her attend a rehearsal or send recordings of rehearsals for producer feedback.
		Last group rehearsal before recording start date. You must have your arrangements locked in by the end of this session. Maybe you'll be inspired to make small changes once you start recording, but you can't count on that: You have to show up with a final, tight version of every song that you can record exactly as written and rehearsed.
		Recording start date.

Recordings Tracker:

Here's an example of a spreadsheet for tracking song ownership for a band recording over several years with various personnel. People and entities represented here include bandmembers, session players, producers receiving points, and the publishing company established collectively by the band.

To adapt this template for yourself, replace ABC, DEF, etc. with each person's actual initials, then add corresponding name and PRO info to the list on right, and add songs as you register them.

Notice that for each song, the songwriter splits, publisher splits, and recording copyrights each add up to 100. Also notice that for the cover song, no songwriter or publisher credits are listed because they belong to the original composer.

If you keep this list up-to-date, decades down the road when you're thinking about your legacy, you'll have a much easier time providing accurate information for your heirs.

Note: These numbers are just examples, not suggested splits. And caution: This is just a tracking document, not a contract or legal guide. There are other elements you might need to track too. Consult with a music attorney to make sure all your bases are covered.

Recordings Tracker:

Song (legal ttl)	Album	BMI Work #	SW ABC	SW DEF	SW GHI	SW JKL	SW MNO	SW PQR	SW STU	SW VWX	Pub1	Pub GHI	Pub ABC	Pub DEF	Pub JKL	Pub MNO	Pub PQR	Pub STU	Pub VWX	Mech ABC	Mech DEF	Mech JKL	Mech MNO	Mech PQR	Mech STU	Mech VWX	Mech YZA	Mech BCD	Mech EFG
Track 1	Album 1	########	55	25	0	10	0	10	0	0	0	0	55	25	10	0	10	0	0	20	20	20	20	20	0	0	0	0	0
Track 2	Album 1	########	55	25	0	10	0	10	0	0	0	0	55	25	10	0	10	0	0	20	20	20	20	20	0	0	0	0	0
Track 3	Album 1	########	65	5	0	10	10	10	0	0	0	0	65	5	10	10	10	0	0	20	20	20	20	20	0	0	0	0	0
Track 4	Album 1	########	65	5	0	10	10	10	0	0	0	0	65	5	10	10	10	0	0	20	20	20	20	20	0	0	0	0	0
Track 5	Album 1	########	55	45	0	0	0	0	0	0	0	0	55	45	0	0	0	0	0	20	20	20	20	20	0	0	0	0	0
Track 6	Album 1	########	35	16.25	0	16.25	16.25	16.25	0	0	0	0	35	16.25	16.25	16.25	16.25	0	0	20	20	20	20	20	0	0	0	0	0
Track 7	Album 1	########	32.50	22.50	0	22.50	0	22.50	0	0	0	0	32.50	22.50	22.50	0	22.50	0	0	20	20	20	20	20	0	0	0	0	0
Track 8	Album 1	########	55	25	0	10	0	10	0	0	0	0	55	25	10	0	10	0	0	20	20	20	20	20	0	0	0	0	0
Track 1	Album 2	########	25	20	0	20	0	10	12.50	12.50	0	0	25	20	20	0	10	12.50	12.50	16	14	14	0	14	14	14	14	0	0
Track 2	Album 2	########	25	20	0	20	0	10	12.50	12.50	0	0	25	20	20	0	10	12.50	12.50	16	14	14	0	14	14	14	14	0	0
Track 3	Album 2	########	25	20	0	20	0	10	12.50	12.50	0	0	25	20	20	0	10	12.50	12.50	16	14	14	0	14	14	14	14	0	0
Track 4	Album 2	########	25	20	0	20	0	10	12.50	12.50	0	0	25	20	20	0	10	12.50	12.50	16	14	14	0	14	14	14	14	0	0
Track 5 (cover)	Album 2	########	0	0	0	0	0	0	0	0	0	0	0	0	0	0	0	0	0	16	14	14	0	14	14	14	14	0	0
Track 6	Album 2	########	30	15	0	25	0	15	7.50	7.50	0	0	35	15	25	0	15	7.50	7.50	16	14	14	0	14	14	14	14	0	0
Track 7	Album 2	########	25	15	0	20	0	15	12.50	12.50	0	0	25	15	20	0	15	12.50	12.50	16	14	14	0	14	14	14	14	0	0
Track 8	Album 2	########	25	20	0	20	0	10	12.50	12.50	0	0	25	20	20	0	10	12.50	12.50	16	14	14	0	14	14	14	14	0	0
Track 1	EP 1	########	55	35	10	0	0	0	0	0	90	10	0	0	0	0	0	0	0	41	41	8	0	0	0	0	0	0	5
Track 2	EP 1	########	45	45	10	0	0	0	0	0	90	10	0	0	0	0	0	0	0	46	46	0	0	0	0	0	0	5	3
Track 3	EP 1	########	46	28	10	16	0	0	0	0	90	10	0	0	0	0	0	0	0	42	41	7	0	0	0	0	0	5	0
Track 4	EP 1	########	45	38	10	7	0	0	0	0	90	10	0	0	0	0	0	0	0	47	46	7	0	0	0	0	0	0	0
Track 5	EP 1	########	46	30	10	14	0	0	0	0	90	10	0	0	0	0	0	0	0	42	41	7	0	0	0	0	0	5	0
Single 1	n/a	########	25	15	0	15	10	10	12	13	0	0	25	15	15	10	10	12	13	16	14	14	14	14	0	0	0	0	0
Single 2	n/a	########	25	15	0	15	10	10	13	12	0	0	25	15	15	10	10	13	12	16	14	14	14	14	0	0	0	0	0

Songwriters/Performers

Songwriters/Performers	PRO	CAE/IPI #
[Name of Person ABC]	BMI	########
[Name of DEF]	BMI	########
[Name of [GHI]	ASCAP	########
[Name of JKL]	BMI	########
[Name of MNO]	BMI	########
[Name of PQR]	ASCAP	########
[Name of STU]	BMI	########
[Name of VWX]	BMI	########
[Name of YZA]	SESAC	########
[Name of BCD]	ASCAP	########
[Name of EFG]	SESAC	########

Publishers	PRO	CAE/IPI #
[Name of Pub]	BMI	########

161

Sync Licensing Tracker:

Here's an example that's similar to the previous Recordings Tracker, but focused on the tasks of uploading songs to a sync licensing database such as MusicSupervisor.com. You could make one giant spreadsheet combining both (which is actually what I do, but I broke it out into two so it would fit on these pages).

I created this as a spreadsheet to make it easily sortable by song title, album, release date, etc. Since this one is a work in progress, some boxes have checkmarks (indicating completed) and some don't. Similar to the PR columns of the Master Schedule spreadsheet, this makes it easy to spot which tasks still need to be done.

Under "Versions Uploaded," V = vocals and N = the no-vocals version of the same song.

Sync Licensing Tracker:

Song (legal title)	Album	Original Release Date	Versions Uploaded	Song Info	Search Info	Lyrics	Storyline, Pitch	Live in Catalog
Title 1	Album 1 title		Y, N	✓	✓	✓	✓	✓
Title 2	Album 1 title		Y, N	✓	✓			
Title 3	Album 1 title		Y, N	✓	✓			
Title 4	Album 1 title		Y, N	✓	✓	✓	✓	✓
Title 5	Album 1 title		Y, N	✓				
Title 6	Album 1 title		Y, N	✓	✓	✓	✓	✓
Title 7	Album 1 title		Y, N	✓				
Title 8	Album 1 title		Y, N	✓				
Title 9	Album 2 title		✓	✓	✓	✓	✓	✓
Title 10	Album 2 title		✓	✓	✓	✓	✓	✓
Title 11	Album 2 title		✓	✓	✓	✓	✓	✓
Title 12	Album 2 title		✓	✓	✓	✓	✓	✓
Title 13	Album 2 title		✓	✓	✓	✓	✓	✓
Title 14	Album 2 title		✓	✓	✓	✓	✓	✓
Title 15	Album 2 title		✓	✓	✓	✓	✓	✓
Title 16	Album 2 title		✓	✓	✓	✓	✓	✓
Title 17	Album 3 title		Y, N	✓	✓	✓	✓	✓
Title 18	Album 3 title		Y, N	✓	✓	✓	✓	✓
Title 19	Album 3 title		Y, N	✓	✓	✓	✓	✓
Title 20	Album 3 title		Y, N	✓	✓	✓	✓	✓
Title 21	Album 3 title		Y, N	✓	✓	✓	✓	✓
Title 22	n/a–single		✓	✓				
Title 23	n/a–single		✓	✓				

Performing & Production

This section includes examples of a stage plot with inputs, a gear inventory, and a checklist for self-producing shows. That last one might seem like an impossibly complex undertaking, but with all of the other tools and organizational strategies you now have, it's well within your ability.

A word about setlists:

Setlists are the most obvious item under this heading. Some of you generate computer printouts; most of you hand-write them in Sharpie. Some of you stick with them religiously; others change them mid-set to adapt to the vibe of the crowd or your own feel for how the show is flowing. Some of you don't use setlists at all.

I say, do what works for you and your band. But I'll throw in a couple points to consider: If you have a setlist, after the show you can quickly note any variations you made mid-stream, add the date and venue name, and you'll have an easy record of which songs you can submit to receive performance royalties for performing your own originals live. (Yes, you can do that— read up on how it works with your performing rights organization). Also, spare copies make great fan gifts. Sometimes they'll even grab them from the stage, so if you don't want to lose your copy, you better grab it first.

Stage Plot with Inputs:

You'll need this repeatedly, so why not stop sketching it on cocktail napkins? Up the professionalism and eliminate having to do it over and over by creating it once in a drawing or graphic design app.

Include key details, such as make and model of equipment if relevant or unusual variations (such as the lead vox setup as noted here). Be sure to include your contact info on the image, and also include the "Last updated" date in case the sound engineer has an old one of yours from the last time you played there.

Make multiple versions if you use different setups depending on the show. Then save them as photos on your phone to easily email or text on the fly.

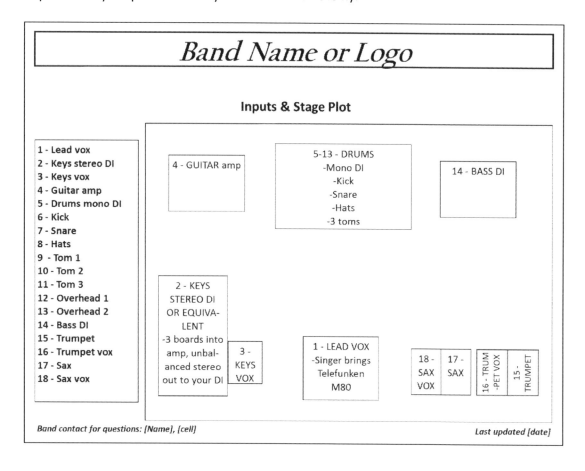

Gear Inventory:

Nobody wants to think about getting robbed, but you know it happens. You probably know someone it happened to. Use a list like this to prepare for the worst.

Don't feel like you have to create a comprehensive list in one take. Start on it now with whatever items come to mind and continue filling in details and adding more items over time. That dead waiting period between soundcheck and stage is a good time to add to this inventory.

List absolutely every piece of gear that each of you owns or has on extended loan: Instruments, cases, stands, laptops, tablets, cables, pedals, connectors, accessories—everything. If you wish, include gear that never travels and let the list protect against home burglary as well as theft on the road or from your rehearsal space.

In the "Replacement Value" column, list the amount it would cost you to buy the exact same item or something that functions the same, whichever amount is higher. For example, if you have a guitar that is worth $5,000, list $5,000 as the replacement value; if you have a guitar that you scored at a garage sale for $10, list the replacement value as whatever it would cost you to get a decent, similar guitar (maybe $200-$300). For wearable or frequently replaced items like strings and sticks, add a line to represent the value of the quantity you normally carry with you.

Take multiple photos of each item from different angles, and get close-ups on any distinguishing features. Save the photos in cloud storage so you can access them from anywhere.

Print out the entire completed list (make sure the info in each column is fully visible) and use the last column to create a tour inventory. If you're driving, check items in as each member arrives before loading the van. If you're flying, have each member mark the items s/he checked as baggage or is carrying on. When everything is checked in, take a photo of each page with your phone. If the worst happens, you can simply hand the paper list to the police and use the photographed pages for insurance claims.

You might find local uses for this list as well. Festivals and other quick-turn multi-act showcases are fertile ground for thieves and for innocent mistakes. If you have people willing to help you haul your gear but you've been afraid to let go and trust their memory over yours, here's your solution: Have them check in and out with this list.

Bonus tip:

Use white or yellow gaff tape and Sharpie to label every case, bag, and freestanding item with your band name. This won't deter thieves, of course, but it will make it harder to overlook items during load-out.

Gear Inventory:

ITEM	MAKE	MODEL	COLOR	SERIAL #	APPROX AGE	DATE ACQUIRED	ACQUIRED FROM	REPLACE-MENT VALUE	PHOTOS ON FILE?	DETAILS [Distinguishing features like scratches, custom pickups, strap design]	OWNER	ON TOUR [DATE]
guitar								$				
case, guitar								$				
guitar								$				
case, guitar								$				
ukelele								$				
case, uke								$				
bass guitar								$				
case, bass								$				
bass-upright								$				
case, upright bass								$				
keyboard								$				
case, keyboard								$				
drum, kick								$				
drum, tom								$				
drum, snare								$				
cymbal								$				
saxophone								$				
trumpet								$				
trombone								$				
tambourine								$				
microphone								$				
mic stand								$				
amp								$				
bass cabinet								$				
PA								$				
loop station								$				
pedal								$				
cable								$				
music stand								$				
iPad								$				
tuner								$				
guitar slide								$				

Show Self-Production Checklist:

This one pulls together elements of several of the previous chapters as well as other tools in this chapter to help you to get your mind around the complexities of producing your own multi-act event. It can be terrifying and stressful, but running your own show is the epitome of indie-artist empowerment, so, when you feel ready (or as ready as you'll ever be), I encourage you to do it.

You don't have to also perform in your productions, particularly if you want to try one or a few to get your bearings without also having to worry about your own set. However, once you get a taste for it, you might find that not much compares to the satisfaction of headlining an event that spotlights your act while providing a discovery showcase for several younger acts, cross-pollinating each band's audiences, and pulling fresh media attention as most likely the town's biggest event of the night.

The checklist on the next page lists key tasks involved in producing your own event. As with all of the tools in this book, you must add to, change, and customize it to make it exactly what you need.

Give yourself at least three months to pull a show together. More time is better, but it's understood that some components can't be known or decided that far in advance. A 3- to 4-month window is tight but doable for a single-night, single-location event with up to 5 acts. Elements such as permitting, heavy sponsor reliance, paid PR, and custom stage construction require even more lead time ... best to get your feet wet with a club-level production.

Show Self-Production Checklist:

Funding
- Draft your event budget. Will you need to pay a rental fee for the venue or will they accept a percentage of the door? How much can you afford to pay your bands? How much budget do you have for social media ads and other paid promotion? Also consider staffing expenses such as sound engineer, photographer/videographer, and door staff if not provided by the venue.

Venue
- Scout and choose your venue. Determine the terms of the event: Is this a venue rental or a standard club night? If there is a contract, read it line for line and be sure you understand it.
- Once terms are agreeable, hold the date in anticipation of booking confirmations (below).
- If outdoors, consider whether you need rented tents or rainout insurance.
- Does your event need food? Does the venue have it? What are your options for food trucks or catering?
- Does your venue sell alcohol? If not, can you bring on a drink sponsor? Budget for a certified bartender if needed.
- What backline if any is provided by the venue or the sound company? Is there any equipment that you will need to rent?

Booking
- Scout, choose, and book other acts. Set payment terms up front, whether guarantee, door split, or combo. Get their agreement to your requirements for promotion (below). Get the name, phone, and email of your contact for each band.
- When the bill is solid enough (i.e. a few anchor acts and good options for filling any remaining slots), confirm the date with the venue. Pay the deposit if applicable.
- Get stage plots/inputs from all bands.

Promotion
- Plan event promo (see Event Promotion Grid).
- Involve the other acts in promotion. Give them clear expectations regarding their contributions to postering, social media posting, direct invitations, etc. (As the producer, you will typically take responsibility for any paid promotion, but every act on the bill should pull their weight with social media, press interviews/appearances, and relational promo.)
- Work the plan all the way through the day after the show.

Pix/Vid
- Are you hiring a photographer or videographer? If so, clarify which bands are to be included. This is a good opportunity for newer bands to receive high-quality live assets, and the photographer might be willing to offer a discount if more than one band buys in. (This is not an expense you as the producer would be expected to carry unless the output is for your use alone.)
- Will you be livestreaming? All bands, some, or just yours? Make sure this is clear to all performers and to the person(s) operating the camera/managing the stream.

Hospitality and Retail
- Identify the green room space, or create one. Ensure water will be available for all performers. Decide in advance whether snacks and drink or meal tickets will be provided for performers. Also determine guest-list parameters.
- Identify the merch space, or create one. Coordinate merch sales among all acts to ensure everyone has the space they need.

Run of Show
- Well in advance, define the roles of each person involved and secure staff or volunteers for each role. If you are also performing, you are strongly encouraged to deputize someone else as the show-runner. This person will be responsible for arriving early, supervising load-in and retail setup, greeting and directing all performers as they arrive, keeping each act on time, ensuring everyone else is doing their jobs and resolving any problems during the event, and settling the payout with the venue, contractors, and each act at the end of the night.
- At least one week before the event, email an advance with all details including venue location and load-in/soundcheck times to all performers, staff, and volunteers.
- Check in with all staff and volunteers the day before the event to confirm they know their jobs and arrival times.
- Arrive early, even if you're not the show-runner, get set up, and then work the plan. If you're performing, let the show-runner do his or her job so you can get your head in the game and put on a great show.

AFTERWORD

Remember that being organized means continually adapting and evolving. All of the templates and samples in the last chapter are only starting points to help you create a basis for your own systems. It's fine, and good in fact, to keep changing as your needs change. If you find that you're refining your checklists every time you use them, congrats: You're doing it right.

Further resources:

There are thousands of other books, blogs, websites, podcasts, and people who have valuable things to say about organization, professional musicianship, and the music industry in general. If I had tried to list them all here, this book would have been outdated before it was published.

Instead I encourage you to become a skilled researcher. Look up the people and sources I've quoted throughout the book. Get into the habit of making informed decisions: Search the internet or ask someone you trust, consider a variety of perspectives, then move forward. Don't let indecision paralyze you. Part of being organized is balancing planning and action. The "right answer" will come from your own investigation, analysis, and, when appropriate, the strategic use of experts such as an attorney, accountant, or business consultant.

If you want my help directly, contact me through my website: ThoughtsInOrder.com. I offer hourly consulting at not-outrageous rates.

Keep up the convo on social media:

By now I've probably already thought of things I wish I'd included in this book. I'll be continuing the conversation on my social media by sharing more of my own thoughts, plus new insights from musicians and industry folks, and I invite you to join in with your own ideas and questions. Follow me on Facebook at www.facebook.com/ThoughtsInOrder and on Twitter at @DebStanleyTIO.

INDEX

Made in the USA
San Bernardino, CA
21 February 2017